A **Path**
Power
to

A Master's Guide.
to Conquering Crisis

Mack Newton
with Michele St. George

NTKD
Publishing

Published by:
NTKD Publishing
3243-A East Indian School Road, Phoenix Arizona 85018

Cover photograph by Karen Shell,
Shell Photographics, Phoenix, Arizona

Printed in the United States of America
First Printing October 1997
10 9 8 7 6 5 4 3 2 1

Publisher's Cataloging-in-Publication
Newton, Mack.
    A path to power : a master's guide to conquering crisis / Mack Newton with Michele St. George. — 1st ed.
    p. cm.
    ISBN: 0-9659821-3-0
1. Self-actualization (Psychology) 2. Self-help techniques.
I. Title.

BF637.S4N49 1997   158.1
                                    QBI97-41061

In loving memory of my mother,
Ruby Newton

Contents

Acknowledgments

In acknowledging the people who deserve credit, let me start with Michele St. George, my co-author, who took piles of notes and hours upon hours of audio recordings of my speeches and turned it into a book.

Sometimes it seems to me that I've lived several lives and met and been influenced by hundreds of people over the years. My thanks to all those who, knowingly or unknowingly, left an imprint on my life.

I want to thank Brian Tracy for his inspiration and encouragement during a period of suffering I thought would never end. Brian opened my eyes to my possibilities and opportunities, probably without ever realizing his effect on me. I've also been greatly influenced by the writings of Nathaniel Branden, Price Pritchett, Ph.D. and Og Mandino. I'm indebted to Fred Alan Wolf, Ralph Waldo Emerson and Victor Frankl, whose thoughts, writing and philosophies have inspired me over the years.

Thanks also to my students and clients who supplied me with articles, books and reprints to read, absorb, and discuss. My Black Belt student, Nick Kapande, encouraged me to become a speaker with Peak Performers Network and wouldn't let me rest until I got started.

Foreword

Throughout the course of history there have been special individuals who have greatly impacted the lives of millions of people and in some cases have even changed the course of history. These special individuals seem to have a great amount of energy that radiates from them. People are attracted to them to *feel* their presence. Their goal is to come away with a sense of renewal, revitalization, insight, inspiration or rebirth.

Many people have been physically and mentally crippled with pain either from a tragic accident, sports injury, or other health challenge. Those same people are now healthy and alive with more energy and vitality than at any previous time in their lives. They are very diverse in age, income, social status, profession, and ethnic background, What they all have in common is that they were inspired and rehabilitated by Mack Newton.

It was during spring training in 1986 while visiting with one of my clients who played for the Oakland A's that I first met Mack Newton. He was the A's physical conditioning coach. I remember seeing him for the first time vividly. He walked into training camp with large dark sunglasses and his boom box. Mack always conducts his workouts to music. His arrival and presence was so impressive that it reminded me of Darth Vader's grand entrance in the first *Star Wars* movie when everyone in the theater let out a "woo" in unison.

I was astounded at the amount of respect that the players had for Mack. Even though some of the players were half his age and some were superstars, it was obvious that none of them were close to his level of physical presence. They worked very hard under his stern direction. His workout technique was unique. I wanted to experience this very different workout regimen for myself. A few days later, positioning myself about 15 yards from the team, I did the entire workout with them. I still cannot explain why but for some reason I really wanted him to see me complete his workout.

Suddenly to my surprise I saw something that I had never seen before. I saw Mack looking in my direction, *smiling*! I turned around to see who was behind me, but there was no one. I looked back and Mack pointed to me and gave me his characteristic thumbs up sign. The sense of accomplishment that came over me at that moment is the reason why people from all walks of life, from children to senior citizens, professional athletes to weekend warriors, executives and laborers, all come to Phoenix to work out with the master, Mack Newton.

Over the years during my visits to Phoenix to train with Mack, I have seen people who were in tremendous pain from hip replacements and various physical problems exercising beside professional athletes. When their legs shook violently from exhaustion (we've all been there with Mack) and they collapsed on the floor, somehow, some way Mack was able to get another 200 mountain climbers and 50 pushups from them. But more impressive than the additional push-ups was the look of accomplishment and zest for life on their faces when they looked up at Mack as he smiled approvingly.

The ancient Egyptians taught science and religion using metaphors, allegories, and symbolism. They believed that there are many aspects to the human psyche and gave them names and faces along with stories, or myths of how they interacted with each other. These characters or gods as some refer to them were called the *Neters* which translates to *"forces of nature."*

Have you ever heard stories of how a small woman lifted a 3000 pound car off of her child? Or someone who risks their life in an heroic way and performs with incredible strength and courage? These people are acting out of that part of our human psyche that the ancient Egyptians called Heru, from which the word hero was later derived. Although Mack has mastered the movements and workings of the human body, I believe that it is his ability to awaken the hero in all of us to perform far beyond the limitations that we set for ourselves that makes him a great Master.

In 1990, I was diagnosed with a rare blood disorder. My doctor advised me of possible major organ failure if my blood count continued to drop. I was in a lot of pain, my body was covered with black and blue marks, and I was constantly nauseous. My business had taken a major downturn and I was going through a very painful divorce. I was depressed.

Mack told me to come and train with him. I tried to explain to him that I could not afford to spend a month in Phoenix. He assured me in his voice that speaks with great confidence as well as compassion that all I had to do was get there and not to worry about anything else. I flew to Phoenix the next day. Three weeks later I left with my blood count back to normal, practically all of the black and blue marks gone, and more energy and enthusiasm than I had ever felt in my life. Although he humbly downplays his role, I truly believe he saved my life.

There is a saying that goes: Those who can *do* and those who can't *teach*. Mack Newton is the combination of a great teacher as well as one who has overcome more physical and life challenges than most of us can even imagine. He is the physical manifestation of Heru and a living example of the greatness and capability of the human spirit.

There are thousands who could give testimonials of how their lives were saved or greatly enriched by going to Phoenix to train with the Master.

This guide can help you to achieve many of those benefits in lieu of being there. Take your time reading it. Experience it. Live and do the things that Mack recommends. Join the thousands of us who live life more abundantly because he has helped to awaken the Heru within us.

Regardless of your goals, you will be energized, motivated and experience a sense of renewal when you finish this guide. And it will be there for you to read again and again, each time gaining more insight and inspiration.

I hope this is only the first published work of many more to come. If it is, the world will be a healthier, happier and a better place for us all.

Pil Sung,

Gene Baynes, CFP
President
G. Baynes & Associates
Centreville, Virginia

1
Taking On Life

Life's fulfillment finds constant contradictions in its path;
but those are necessary for the sake of its advance....
The spirit of fight belongs to the genius of life.
—Rabindranath Tagore

Imagine yourself waking early one morning and studying your reflection in the mirror. Ask yourself: "What challenges do I face today? What circumstances are manipulating my life? Perhaps you are struggling in a chaotic relationship or your career is faltering or finances dwindling, or your health is deteriorating. Or maybe you have reached a state of powerless passivity from too many demands and never enough time.

Fix your gaze firmly on your reflection for a moment longer. *You are confronting the most powerful enemy you will ever encounter.* If you know how to challenge and transform that person staring back at you in the mirror, you create an indomitable power that can roar in the face of defeat, failure or loss: *I will survive and I will thrive.*

1

Inside you is what the poet Tagore referred to as the Spirit of fight. You have an incredible force within you that will overcome anything that is thrown at you. Call it consciousness, mental power, the grace of God, or soul—use whatever name you like, but realize that when your body, mind and spirit is working in harmony *for you* instead of *against you*—you will discover an audacity and strength that will astound you.

It is my firm belief that it is your mission on earth to succeed, to use all your talents, to be a success organism if you like. Every defeat and crisis in your life contains the seeds for a new goal, a new journey, a new adventure.

Why Do You Need Power?

The mere mention of the word *power* often scares the pants off people. We've been trained from childhood to mistrust our own power. Brute power is so often misused, it corrupts, it asserts its authority over others. Hitler, Nero and Mussolini had power. Yet so did Gandhi, Jesus, Mother Teresa and Martin Luther King Jr. Power is simply another of the universe's energies. How you use it shapes the difference between creation and destruction.

> *Spiritual force is stronger than material force; thoughts rule the world.*
> —Ralph Waldo Emerson

Inner power arises from the ability to understand mental, physical and spiritual laws—then work in harmony with them to direct events rather than using crude force.

Without power, you are tossed about helplessly in the maelstrom of life's events. You become resentful, fearful and hostile to the changes in your life. With personal power, you wake up fired and ready to take on the world. You learn to cooperate with and incorporate change when it occurs.

Crises become the problems you eat for breakfast.

With undisciplined power, there are only winners and losers, predators and prey. With authentic inner power, you radiate an intuitive knowledge and compassion. Your attitude becomes a magnet for others, influencing them to realize their own strengths. There are no losers.

If we really want to live, we should start at once to try; if we don't it doesn't matter, we'd better start to die.

—W.H. Auden

The purpose of this book is to guide you down a path of self-knowledge and attainment that will empower you to face that person in the mirror without fear or doubt, with the quiet assurance and positive attitude of someone who can say: "I know who I am and what I am capable of accomplishing. I am in control of my life."

Facing Challenges

Many pitfalls lay in your path. Life can be difficult and at times incredibly cruel. You may even feel ambivalent about what you really want, riddled with inner doubt about what you can accomplish, trying to make sense of your life. Your opposing dreams, fears, hopes and doubts become armies clashing in the night. Your inner conflicts spark all your outer conflicts with a spouse, children, parents, a boss.

This is not a book about how to make someone fall in love with you, how to get your boss to appreciate you, or how to get people to like you and respect you. These will occur naturally as you find your own inner power, but they cannot be forced or finessed. Attempts to manipulate events or other people will always flounder. The only person you can change is *you*. This book will teach you to fall in love with yourself and with life. As you transform your inner self, the outer

3

world will change its response to you.

Through forty years in the martial arts I have learned and applied the ancient wisdom of Taekwon-Do, as well as what might be called the modern Western technology of quantum thinking.

Taekwon-Do, which is a Korean martial art, demands long hours of physical conditioning to acquire the proficiency of a master. Its code of conduct is rigorous as well. The student aspires to five basic tenets: *Integrity, Perseverance, Courtesy, Self-Control* and *Indomitable Spirit.* Practicing these tenets assures not only physical skill, but mental mastery as well. When I was a young black belt and seeking to become a world champion, my instructor gave me a valuable piece of advice: "It is not important to become a superior fighter, but to become a superior thinker." When this important principle becomes rooted in your soul, you will realize that the present is the result of your past thoughts, and that everything you can become in the future is dependent on your thoughts *now.*

Quantum physics is the powerful science that made space technology possible, along with computers, lasers, and modern electronics. A quantum leap is the explosive jump that a particle of matter undergoes in moving from one level of functioning to another. When making this leap it can skip many stops in between with no apparent effort. Quantum thinking is a way to arrive at new ideas and solutions through similar leaps in consciousness. It requires a letting go of old thinking that grinds us into archaic and ineffective methods of progress. We all do things that don't work anymore, but we continue to do them because they have worked in the past, or we are comfortable with them, or we don't know any different way of doing things. Quantum thinking gives you the chance to make that bold and direct leap to solutions.

Philosophy and science can be distilled into a powerful mental technology that is a blueprint to personal power and peak performance, whether as an athlete or business professional, a parent or spouse. It's not mystical, it's not magical thinking or a quick-fix for what ails you. It does require considerable effort on your part. It will empower you to face all of life's storms head on, as master of your own ship.

Who Do You Want To Be?

It's a good sign that you have reached for this book. If you feel the first stirrings of this inner power crouching within your soul, you have received your wake-up call. You are at the beginning of an evolutionary breakthrough.

This book will introduce a path to power that will awaken your inner might. I don't say this as a matter of blind faith or optimism. Examples in this book are drawn not from theory, but from the flesh-and-blood victories of myself and hundreds of my students.

In my years of self-training, as well as years spent in peak performance training of athletes, children, men and women with

In the depth of winter, I finally learned that within me there lay an invincible summer.

—Albert Camus

debilitating arthritis and other physical traumas, I've discovered a few secrets that I would like to share with you.

My students range from ages four to seventy. Doctors routinely refer patients to me for many kinds of rehabilitation. I've been able to explore my theories on peak performance with athletes such as Bo Jackson and Neil Lomax, with the Oakland A's and the Dallas Cowboys, with dancers and business professionals, with men and women crippled with a progressive form of arthritis called ankylosing spondilitis, with children and teenagers struggling with the desire for self-worth and personal power in a violent society.

Age is no barrier to power. Just a couple of students who have discovered their own inner strength include a 65-year-old grandmother who rebounded from the crippling effects of arthritis and turned back the clock on her own aging process, losing eighty pounds in the process, and a 67-year-old survivor of illium cancer who now walks independently after radical surgery left her in a wheelchair. Their physical rehabilitation varies tremendously according to their needs. The mental principles by which they overcome their defeat and find their path to power is *100% the same in every instance.*

It has been my job in life to chase my dreams, no matter what defeat life dealt me. It's your job too. It's the only way you're going to be satisfied. It's the only way to feel fulfilled. It's never too late.

True power can only result from forging a balanced body-mind-spirit. Mind is the crucial link. Many people believe that their thoughts

> *Life is no brief candle to me. It is sort of a splendid torch which I have got hold of for a moment, and I want to make it burn as brightly as possible before handing it on to future generations.*
>
> —George Bernard Shaw

6

are meaningless, random chatter, mental vignettes appearing on the video screens of their minds. Nothing could be further from the truth.

Thoughts create reality. Ralph Waldo Emerson said we become what we think about all day. Your dominant thoughts literally predict your future, whether positive or negative. Whatever you think about on a consistent basis is programmed directly into your subconscious mind, creating the basis for your actions and your ideas.

Just as compelling is the fact that you are creating reality *for other people* in your sphere by your positive or negative expectations of them. Nothing can be more powerful than simply expecting the best of your spouse, loved ones, and especially your children.

Far better it is to dare mighty things, to win glorious triumphs even though checkered by failure, than to rank with those poor spirits who neither enjoy nor suffer much because they live in the gray twilight that knows neither victory nor defeat.
—Theodore Roosevelt

Your mind—your mindset—is not beyond your control. You are not powerless, you are not a victim of your environment or your own past. Neuroscientific evidence is perfectly clear on this: changing your mindset has the power to transform your life.

Think of something you haven't done yet. Something that will change your life. You know what it is, you just need the courage to take it out and look at it. Even the degree to which you are successful right now may be playing down to your talent. You may be flying too low to the ground, playing it safe. Your comfort zone is a rut.

The secret to bursting out of a rut is to recognize that you are in the same situation again and do something different in the future. You can't keep doing the same thing and expecting different results. It's one of the definitions of insanity. Quantum thinking demands that you become ruthless about finding new ways—*different ways*—to get where you're going.

Here's an autobiography in five short chapters about how I dug out of my own rut:

Chapter One:
I walk down the street. There's a deep hole in the sidewalk and I fall in. I'm lost. It's dark, and it feels hopeless. It's not my fault. It seems to take forever to find a way out.

Chapter Two:
I walk down the same street. There's a deep hole in the sidewalk. I pretend I don't see it. I fall in again. I can't believe I'm back in the same place. It's dark. It's not my fault and it still takes an awful long time to get out.

Chapter Three:
I walk down the same street. There's a deep hole in the sidewalk. I see it's there. I still fall in. It's a habit. This time my eyes are open. I know where I am and realize it is my fault. I get out more quickly.

Chapter Four:
I walk down the same street. There's a deep hole in the sidewalk. I walk around it.

Chapter Five:
I walk down another street.

This book is about how to recognize and propel yourself out of that rut into a higher state of inner power. It is about the life changes and mental attitudes that will grant you the success and joy of a life well-lived to its fullest potential. The psychologist Abraham Maslow called it "self-actualization."

I'll tell you my own story and the stories of my students who have taken the quantum leap into personal power. You'll learn how to:

- Acquire the attitude and mindset that insures your success

- Navigate the swamps of anger, fear, guilt and other negative emotions

- Cooperate with the life you have been given and discover all your gifts

- Learn at an accelerated rate

- Negotiate the often conflicting advice of doctors and experts

- Understand the unique problems of men and women in today's society

- Like yourself and become emotionally self-reliant

- Give and receive love in your personal relationships

- Take control of your own life and future

Our deepest fear is not that we are inadequate.
Our deepest fear is that we are
powerful beyond measure.
It is our light, not our darkness that frightens us.
We ask ourselves, who am I to be brilliant,
gorgeous, talented and fabulous?
You are a child of God.
Your playing small doesn't serve the world.
There's nothing enlightened
about shrinking so that other people
won't feel insecure around you.
You were born to manifest
the glory of God within us.
It's not just in some of us:
It's in everyone.
And as we let our own light shine,
we unconsciously give other people permission
to do the same.
As we are liberated from our own fear,
our presence automatically liberates others.
Nelson Mandela, 1994

2
The Wake-Up Call

Life is either a daring adventure, or it is nothing.
—Helen Keller

I leaped out of the helicopter onto the rain-drenched soil at Quang Nai. Vietnam was approaching its monsoon season and cloudbursts were nearly constant. My damp uniform clung to me in the soggy heat.

A powerful blow to my back sent me reeling into the mud. As I turned around to see who had kicked me, I realized that my worst fear was staring me down. I tried to identify where the mortar shell had hit me. My left side felt numb. The twisted sole of my foot stared back at me. As I unlaced my boot and pulled it down, bones popped out like little chopsticks and spurted blood at me. I pulled my boot back over the shattered foot and started to pray.

Flares of light exploded and my vision blurred. A second concussion grenade ripped into my knees and lower intestine. A 30-caliber bullet ricocheted off my right cheekbone. I sat dumbfounded in a mud hole clutching my belly, now a bloody gash filled with dirt, shrapnel and protruding viscera.

This was the moment I had been fearing and yet somehow strangely

11

expecting for all my nineteen years of life. Fear to me was this: fear was being afraid of the dark, of dogs, new kids, new places, anything that was different. Most of all I was afraid of death, of dying. It had always held a morbid fascination for me. How would I meet my end?

The army provided an escape from living on the streets of Chicago. Now I had a bed with clean sheets and a place to stay. But when I was sent to Vietnam in 1964, I was so paralyzed by fear that I didn't know if I would be able to fire my gun. Death was everywhere. The smell was in the air. Bullets creased the side of the helicopter on one of my first flights. My heart stopped with every resounding blast.

> Character cannot be developed in ease and quiet. Only through experience of trial and suffering can the soul be strengthened, vision cleared, ambition inspired, and success achieved.
>
> —Helen Keller

Charlie Greer had tried to help me with my fear. Eight years older than me and infinitely more mature, he became a surrogate father and best friend. Charlie looked like he was always smiling, or with his black mustache tilting slightly at the edges, like he was ready to burst into a grin. Nearly through his second tour of duty in Vietnam, he was ready to go home to his prized 1957 Chevrolet. Still he took the time to teach me guitar and about electronics and about women. When I went to Vietnam I was still a virgin. Charlie was the only one who knew. He didn't laugh at me, he just told me what to do. He explained to me how to make love to a woman, then arranged my first sexual encounter.

Since Charlie was a support person, he normally didn't go out in the field. One day we were both asked to ride along on a chopper mission because there was a shortage of door gunners. A 50-caliber slug ripped through the fuselage of the Hughie and I turned to see Charlie with a red hole under his chin and the top half of his head exploded into his flight helmet. As I watched Charlie die through my tears, I saw his blood spattered on my shoes and knew that I couldn't be far behind.

Now sprawled in that mud hole in the rain, I was finally staring my own death in the face. At that moment a strange discovery revealed itself : Death is not scary at all. I suppose I was in shock, but I no longer felt any pain or fear. Just very drowsy, as if I could drift off to sleep. Just rest. Death invited me gently, "Hey Mack, come on in."

With a sudden shock I realized that I couldn't go through that door yet. I had never really lived. Fear had always driven me,

> *Man transcends death by finding meaning in his life....*
> *It is the burning desire for the creature to count....*
> *What man really fears is not so much extinction, but extinction with insignificance.*
>
> —Ernest Becker

sending me scurrying for cover. For the first time in my life, as I lay in that mud hole, I wanted to *live*. I wanted to know what life could be like if I was not afraid of everything I encountered. I wanted control over my own life and destiny.

So I called out. I spit the mud and blood and tissue out of my mouth and called *Help! Help*. A medic—I've never known his name— ran onto the battlefield in a barrage of gunfire and pulled me to safety.

Although my decision to live was inspired by a dramatic life-or-death encounter, I still face that same decision every day. So do you.

A Journey Begins

George Bernard Shaw said that "the true joy in life is to be used for a purpose recognized by yourself as a mighty one...being a force of nature instead of a feverish selfish little clod of ailments and grievances complaining that the world will not devote itself to making you happy."

I certainly didn't start out as a force of nature. When I returned to the U.S. from Vietnam, I had three years in a VA Hospital to second-guess my decision to live. All the surgery and physical therapy couldn't mend my shattered hips and knee. My dream of a future career as a martial artist seemed impossible. I wasn't even sure I'd walk again. I sat on a shelf, watching the world pass me by.

Every day I stared out the window at almost anybody walking down the street and thought "Let me have your life—just because you can walk." I would have gladly traded places with any dope addict, any bum or derelict.

I reflected on my life up to that point. Had it ever had any real point or purpose? Was there any reason for me being here?

Voices

My earliest memories are of sitting on the front porch in Jamaica with my great grandmother weaving colorful tales for me. We huddled together inside every time the great monsoons howled and shuddered through the streets.

Great-grandma really seemed to enjoy talking for hours on end to a shy little boy. "When you were born," she told me, "I picked you up and you looked right back in my eyes like you knew me. There was something different about you from the first time I ever saw you. You are special out of all the children I've ever known." She continued to tell me I'm special all my life, quieting many of the harsher voices that told me otherwise.

I've tried many times to remember my mother's face. She was sixteen years old when she had me and she died three months later. They told me it was due to complications of childbirth, but I've always believed it was heartbreak. My father deserted us before I was born and returned to his home in the U.S.

14

I came to this country from Jamaica at nine years old. Grandmother and great-grandmother, who had been raising me, became ill. Fearing that I would end up in a Jamaican orphanage, they legally pursued my father to take me in. He was a U.S. citizen and working for the government, so he complied.

My father met me at the train, and with a brief welcome, deposited me alone on another train to California. I was shuffled through various homes from California to Arkansas to Detroit, in the custody of families whom my father persuaded to care for me. Finally my father was compelled to take me back into his home. He had a new wife and other children, and I was raised as the much-resented outsider.

My father always told me "Mack, you never finish anything you start. You will never amount to anything." At first I didn't believe him because great-grandma had always assured me I was special, but in time I began to live down to his expectations.

We've all still got those voices from childhood telling us that we weren't "good enough." If you were as fortunate as me in having a voice like my great-grandma who told me I was special, then tune in that voice right now. The first step in facing any crisis is to listen only to positive voices. If there are people right now who are telling you "this is too much for you to handle, it's impossible," then tune out those voices! Turn the volume up so high on every encouraging voice you hear that you can't hear the negative ones.

If you are a parent, recognize your own role in how your children will or will not mature. I've worked with a lot of children, in Taekwon-Do, in homeless shelters, special kids of all kinds who are struggling to overcome the negative influences of their early life.

Now I often look enviously at men in the park, teaching their sons to ride a bike, and wonder what kind of father I would have been. I never fathered a child in my younger years because of my own fears of marriage and of turning out to be the same as my father. It is one of the great regrets of my life.

Going It Alone

After I began living with my father's family again, I became a target for bullies in school. I was small for my age and had a pronounced Jamaican accent. I learned to speak "American" by listening to the radio and I countered the physical threat from the bullies by taking karate lessons, paid for by my after-school jobs.

When I was 15, I ran away from home and lived on the streets of Chicago. Sometimes I would sleep in gas station restrooms, wrapped around a toilet bowl or urinal, not knowing if I would wake up to someone trying to assault or rape me. Sometimes I'd sleep in someone's back yard, which seemed safer but then I'd wake up with leeches on my arms that I had to burn off with matches.

Yet I continued going to school, even while living on the street. Something inside me preferred to fend for myself rather than endure the "protection" of people who were abusing me. You've got to be willing to fight for yourself just because you're you. Don't ever accept any kind of abuse.

Get Up and Walk

As I languished in my hospital bed debating my future and past, I got very used to the sympathy that came my way. Nurses, friends, everyone offered consolation and compassion. "Well, Mack, you've had a tough life. It's really tough, it's really too bad." It's easy to get addicted to sympathy, addicted to people telling us how justified we are in suffering and how this is the only life we could be expected to live. It was intoxicating. I loved sympathy.

One day a short, slight man named Sang Ki Eun arrived at my bedside. He had been sent by the impressive Taekwon-Do master Jung Tae Park whom I had met and practiced with in Vietnam.

"Why are you here in the hospital?" asked Sang Ki Eun matter-of-factly.

"I was shot," I replied, waiting for the sympathy that was due me.

"Why don't you get up and walk?" he inquired. His tone was neither critical nor condescending, simply curious.

"I can't walk. I've been shot." I thought perhaps he didn't understand English too well. He nodded cordially and departed. Sang Ki Eun showed up again about a week later. "Why are you still here? Why don't you leave? Why don't you do something besides wasting away?"

"Because I've been shot!" I shouted at him. If he couldn't see my predicament, then I just wished that he would leave. He returned one more time. "Why don't you get up and get out of here? Jung Tae Park thought you were something special. You don't seem special at all."

"Don't you understand?" I screamed at him. *"I can't walk."*

Martial artists don't suffer whiners gladly. He never became angry or demanding, but he didn't see any point in trying to help someone who would not help himself. "I'm not coming back any more until you stand up and do something for yourself," he informed me and left.

Now I was angry. How dare he say I was nothing special? It still took several more months of thinking and that conversation replayed in my head before finally I got up and left. I got on crutches and found a room at a YMCA on the south side of Chicago for $15 a week.

As I faced an unknown road to recovery, I remembered one of my

> *Let him that would move the world, first move himself.*
> —Socrates

childhood dilemmas in Jamaica. Coming home from playing in the fields one day, the sun blasted the dirt road under my feet and the soil got hotter and hotter. Soon my soles were burning and I dashed off into a grassy field to cool down. I began crying because that road was the only way back home and it was so hot that I could no longer walk on it. I was stuck. I still can't remember how I got home that day, but every time I get stuck somewhere I think about that road.

I was about to begin a lifetime of learning and teaching others to travel the impossible road.

Looking for Answers

Recovery from my injuries was rapid once I left the hospital and began working seriously to come back. I went from crutches to full mobility and then returned to Taekwon-Do in earnest to learn everything it could teach me about body movement and function. I began training at a Taekwon-Do school in Chicago and entering competitions across the country.

June 18 became a symbolic day in my life, for I was shot down in Vietnam on that day in 1965, and I won the World Heavyweight black belt championship in Taekwon-Do on June 18, 1972. I won it again two years later. Between 1972 and 1981, I competed in Karate and Kung-fu tournaments, and won or placed in every major Taekwon-Do championship in America. I discovered I wanted to win real bad and proved to myself that I could amount to something if I had the right attitude. I went back and finished college in Chicago.

Since I was young and healthy, I believed that my hips had healed from the Vietnam injuries. Within a few years, I began experiencing pain and stiffness in my left hip. After x-rays, my doctor informed me "Your hip is degenerating. You're losing joint space." He explained that I had a degenerative form of arthritis that could only get worse.

18

Fear began to descend on me again. Would I end up in a wheel-chair? Taekwon-Do was my life and I would not give it up. I was will-ing to do whatever was necessary to keep working and teaching. I de-vised exercises and stepped up my workouts, but more of the same wouldn't work anymore.

By 1983 my hip had degenerated to a point where I could barely walk and often hobbled along with a cane. I moved to Phoenix for the warmer, drier climate and felt better immediately. I took aspirin for the pain, soon stopped limping, and was able to teach another three years before increasing pain told me I had to do something. Replacing the degenerating hip joint seemed to be the only practical solution. At the time, my future didn't look too bright because the only people receiv-ing artificial hips were in their seventies, eighties, or older. When people in their fifties or younger needed artificial hips, doctors often advised them to live with the pain or else they fused the hip, guaranteeing a lack of mobility.

After extensive research, I finally found an aggressive young sur-geon named Paul Pellicci in New York, who was the first physician that believed that I could get an artificial hip and still go back to Taek-won-Do. In August of 1987, he replaced my left hip.

Dr. Pellicci had an attitude that matched mine. I felt confident in his abilities even though we were both traveling into uncharted terri-tory with no guide to follow.

Taking a Risk

Three months after hip replacement, I stood facing myself in the gymnasium mirror. I saw a forty-two year-old athlete in top condition with a hint of fear in his eyes. I took a deep breath and prepared to do my first full straddle stretch, in which the legs are extended to each side and the chest is lowered to the floor. Doctors had told me that lateral stretching would dislocate the hip. "Don't push it," they warned. "It'll cost you forty thousand dollars of your own money to have the hip replaced again. If you try to go back to full activity, you're going to be back here within two years for another hip."

I replied that at least I would have two good years of living the life I wanted to live. I had studied the models of hips, understood how muscles work, and had done all the preparation to make those muscles strong enough to hold that hip in place. Still, there was an element of fear. Suppose they were right?

I lowered myself slowly into the straddle stretch that day without a trace of pain. Shortly afterwards I gave a public demonstration of Taekwon-Do skills, including breaking boards, patterns and sparring. Now I'm ten years down the road, after a second hip replacement, a rebuilt knee and recently open heart surgery to replace a defective valve caused by childhood rheumatic fever. At 52, I can run, jump, kick and ride my bicycle for 75 miles. I stress-test at age 29. The dream has expanded beyond imagination.

I'm going to share a few secrets with you that I have learned through the years of experimentation on myself as well as the personal victories of my students and clients. I hope that you are able to integrate this mental technology into every area of your life.

Inside you is an extraordinary human being.

3
The Quantum Leap

If we keep doing what we're doing,
we're going to keep getting what we're getting.
—Stephen Covey

Have you ever seen a fly trapped in a window? He wants out. Instinct and experience encourage the fly to "fly harder, fly faster," and so he buzzes in frustration against the unyielding glass. The harder that fly tries, the sooner he will become exhausted and end up dead with the other fly carcasses on the windowsill. Yet across the room is an open door. If the fly would turn 180 degrees in the opposite direction, he could be out the door and free in five seconds of effortless flight.

Like that fly, we often keep butting our heads against the same old obstacles. We work harder and faster at the same jobs, the same toxic relationships, even though they are not producing the results we want. The harder you work at doing things the old way, the faster you approach burnout. It happens in relationships as well as jobs. No matter how hard you try, things don't get better. Unless you can acquire a new vision, a new way of forging ahead, you will either end up ill from the stress, addicted to various forms of escape, or living a life of extended mediocrity.

How do you acquire that new vision? The study of quantum mechanics taught me a way to make mind-boggling leaps in functioning that my students now utilize to do the "impossible."

The relationship between your mind and physical matter is no longer a matter of conjecture or "new age" belief. Quantum physicists— scientists who study matter and energy— have reached some amazing conclusions in their study of the atom. Experimenters have discovered that atomic particles *change when observed*. They may actually *behave in a manner expected by the experimenter.*

The implications of this are astounding. If the human intellect can impact the structures of an atom, then human awareness and the workings of the universe must be inextricably linked. Quantum physics demonstrates that the universe doesn't work like an automaton or machine. It is influenced and changed by the mind that knows how to work in harmony with it.

> *A Human Thought is an actual EXISTENCE, and a Force and Power, capable of acting upon and controlling matter as well as mind.*
> —Albert Pike

The physicist Fred Alan Wolf states that "Quantum mechanics appears to describe a universal order that includes us in a very special way. In fact, our minds may enter into nature in a way we had not imagined possible....The order of the universe may be the order of our own minds."

In other words, you are not a passive observer of what is "out there." Your actions and your mental expectations create physical change in your environment. You will attract people and circumstances to you that are in harmony with your dominant thoughts. A circle of invisible influence exists around you as you read this book.

22

The effect of mind on body is an expanding field in medicine, called psychoneuroimmunology, or PNI. The mind-body effect has also been well known in scientific experimentation. One classic experiment occurred in medical school, when lecturers gave pharmacology students detailed descriptions of how sedatives and stimulants would affect their body. The students were given harmless, inert pills called placebos, but they were told that half would be taking a stimulant and the other half a sedative. They recorded each other's reactions.

> *Like attracts like.*
> *Whatever the conscious mind*
> *thinks and believes,*
> *the subconscious*
> *identically creates.*
> —Brian Adams

About half of the students had measurable symptoms, including a change in blood pressure or heart rate, dizziness or abdominal pain, according to whichever drug they thought they had taken. Like the atomic particles, our bodies change according to what we *think* we will experience.

Placebos can have beneficial effects, but just as often we are drugged by what has been called *no-cebos*, which are our negative expectations based on prior experience. You know firsthand that negative emotions are expressed in the body as well as the mind. If you've ever had a pounding headache from stress at work, lost your voice prior to an important business presentation, or come down with the flu before a vacation, you've experienced the no-cebo effect.

Sometimes athletes tell me that they can't play certain positions because their coach in high school said "You're not fast enough to be an outfielder," or "You're too clumsy to play middle infield You don't have the strength to be a power hitter." They accepted that flawed conclusion then began to live their life in harmony with it.

I experienced the no-cebo effect when I was scheduled to go to

Germany in 1974 to compete in the Taekwon-Do world champion-ships. The expectations for my performance were high because I was the reigning world champion. I had won in 1972 out of nowhere.

Although I knew that I was capable of a lot of things, I did not yet accept in my own mind that I was deserving of good things to happen to me. Rather than compete, I "accidentally" broke my wrist and my hand in two places.

Comfortable with the fact that no one could condemn me for not competing with a broken hand, I went to Germany to watch the matches. There I saw the same competitors, with the same techniques, that I had competed against in the U.S. I knew it would have been possible to win the world championship as well.

Why did I do that to myself? I demanded, in a spontaneous recog-nition of the fact that I had denied myself the opportunity to advance.

The first step to overcoming no-cebos is to develop a *quantum mindset.* You now know that your thinking can create actual change in your world, but how can you develop this ability? How long will it take?

The coming chapters will describe many ways to alter your think-ing to effectively change the results you are getting in life, but first there is one more lesson you can learn from physics, and that is the concept of a *quantum leap.*

Quantum physicists have discovered that electrons often take spon-taneous, explosive leaps to a new energy state. Quantum leaps are not predictable. They cannot be forced, yet all particles of the physical universe must make these unpredictable jumps in space or they will cease to exist.

People can make similar quantum leaps in energy and functioning:

- A smoker fails at all conventional means of quitting. Yet one morning, without conscious effort, she throws away the pack and never smokes again.

- A basketball player suddenly finds himself "in the zone." Despite previous lackluster performances, he makes basket after basket one night, so focused on the hoop that he doesn't hear the roaring approval of the crowd.

- A scientist awakens from a dream one night with a perfectly formed image of how to solve the problem that has baffled him for years.

- A self-effacing, downsized business executive discovers skills that carry her to the top of a completely new profession.

How did they do it? You will note that none of their behaviors were forced. They didn't *make* quantum leaps happen, they *let* them happen.

In other words, your *mindset* is what will determine when you are ready to make one of these unexpected and yet natural leaps in energy and consciousness. A quantum leap is an intuitive, instinctive move which can seem like a miracle. It often happens after a long plateau of unrewarded effort. It is not predictable. It is not rational.

You cannot force a quantum leap, yet you can lay the groundwork for it to occur naturally.

People often believe that success comes one step at a time. The popular notion is that we move systematically from one level of achievement to the next. It's called gradual progress, in which your day-to-day routine brings incremental gains.

However, in certain areas of your life, you can begin skipping levels. You can move from your present level of achievement to one that is several stages higher in a direct breakthrough.

Gains will be exponential rather than incremental. You'll multiply rather than add. Quantum leaps are the elegant solution to a problem, always characterized by these four elements: simplicity, precision, efficiency, neatness.

Everybody has at least one area of their life where a quantum leap is possible right now. You may even have two areas of your life, and a very few may have as many as four possible quantum leaps available. The trick is to figure out where it is. All that's missing is the decision to go for it.

> *Most people can do extraordinary things if they have the confidence or take the risks. Yet most people don't. They sit in front of the telly and treat life as if it goes on forever.*
>
> —Philip Adams

Fred Alan Wolf refers to quantum leaps as venturing into uncharted territory with no guide to follow.

These three steps are necessary to allow a quantum leap to happen:

1: Have an aiming point, a goal.

2: Take action. Get started, even if the details of how to reach your goal aren't apparent yet.

3: Learn from your mistakes and continue the pursuit.

Quantum leaps require an abrupt change in your behavior as well as paradoxical thinking. Here's eight ways to coax your brain into a quantum leap:

Quit trying harder

Like that fly, you cannot make a quantum leap by simply doing more of the same. "To perseverate" is a neuropsychological term which means to persevere in performing an action even when it no longer produces a desired result.

We have faith in the familiar. If you follow the same behavior patterns over and over, you will get better and better at what you've always done. This is not an argument against self-discipline, but generally you will find that trying harder at the old way only produces incremental gains and is a fast road to burnout. It's like driving your car faster and faster in one gear. Sooner or later you will grind to a complete breakdown.

Conventional approaches will bring conventional gains. Reasonable means will produce reasonable results. If you want a higher level of performance, you must seek *unconventional* approaches.

These steps can inspire quantum thinking:

* Think through all the possibilities, consciously work at your problem.

* Research, talk to others, learn any new information you need to know.

* Ask for an answer. *Expect* a breakthrough. Your intuitive right brain will begin reorganizing the information. A flash of inspiration or insight will suddenly arrive out of the blue. The intuitive flash from your unconscious may happen instantly or it may take some period of time, but *it will arrive.* Remain in an expectant mode until it does.

Use this formula to quit trying so hard. The world will resist your efforts to force or manipulate it.

Adopt Risky Behavior

Make no mistake about it, quantum leaps require risk. You can't steal second base by keeping your foot on first. Something is always at stake in life. All you can do is decide which risks you are willing to take.

If you risk nothing, it is the surest way of losing. You will never learn who you are, never stretch or reach. In the end you become rigid, timid, a victim.

If you limit your choices only to what seems possible or reasonable, you disconnect yourself from what you truly want and all that is left is a compromise.

—Robert Fritz

Risk is scary as hell. Sometimes it means letting go of everything you've already got to take a leap into an unknown future. When you break out of normal behavior patterns, you deliberately destabilize yourself.

Be prepared for anxiety, inner chaos or confusion. You will feel clumsy, awkward, uncomfortable and at risk. A high comfort level provides solid evidence that you are playing it safe. If you're experiencing no pain or difficulty, you've probably aimed too low. You may be making gradual progress, but you are not going for a breakthrough.

Yet what will you risk if you don't make that leap? Will you get only a fraction of what life has to offer? A mediocre life of unfulfilled potential?

Jump out of your personal safety zone and test the odds against you!

I'm not telling you to turn your life into a crapshoot. You don't need to be reckless, just determined and committed to change.

Challenge Logic

Western culture relies heavily on logical reasoning and analysis. In school we are taught almost exclusively to think in a linear fashion, drawing conclusions with words and numbers based on what we see, hear and touch. We describe a person who doesn't agree with our obvious conclusions as "irrational."

Intuition and "gut feelings" are also accurate guides to knowledge. Neurological research has shown that your bilateral brain can make effective use of both forms of observation. The holistic combining of logic and intuition is the road to personal knowledge and strength. However, because we have been so thoroughly trained in the logical or rational approach to solutions, our brains may need a tuning workout in the illogical "right brain."

A quantum leap requires paradoxical moves, unusual behavior. A ricochet, an angle suddenly occurs in your thought patterns. The first illogical step is to assume that nothing you have been taught is true, to retest the logic of all your assumptions.

In India they control elephants by tying them to the ground with a small wooden stake and a piece of rope.

The powerful elephant is perfectly capable of pulling out that stake, but trainers imprisoned him as a baby with a chain and deep stake from which he couldn't pull free no matter how hard he tried.

As an adult, the elephant no longer even tries to escape because experience has taught him that it's useless.

> *Man,*
> *surrounded by facts,*
> *permitting himself*
> *no surprise,*
> *no intuitive flash,*
> *no great hypothesis,*
> *no risk,*
> *is in a locked cell.*
> *Ignorance cannot seal*
> *the mind*
> *and imagination*
> *more securely.*
> —Lillian Smith

29

Have you established any personal boundary lines in the same way? You tried once or twice before and failed, so you assume you've discovered your limits. It's a trap you've sprung on yourself. The knowledge that comes from experience can be a curse because it sets a ceiling on how high you can fly. Much of your flawed think may simply arise from habitual thinking. "I've always done it this way and it's comfortable."

Begin focusing on possibilities rather than limitations. Question the truth of what you were taught about yourself as a child. Look at all the "no's" in your life.

What if nothing you have been taught about work, about relationships, about life is true? Suppose you did the complete opposite of what you think you should do?

When I left the V.A. Hospital in Chicago, I had to learn how to walk again because none of their physical therapy had worked. With a combination of desperation and determination, I began experimenting on my own body. Therapists told me not to put stress on my leg, so I put stress on it, forcing myself to walk with my crutches, sometimes even hopping on one leg to gain some speed. They told me to do ten leg extensions every day. I did a thousand, and began adding bicycle kicks. I started getting better real fast.

Don't get the idea that anything is possible. It's not. In some areas of your life, however, what is within your reach is enough to stagger your imagination.

You can double your level of success, you can triple it, go to the second or third or fourth power. There are limits, but they will take care of themselves. Your own personal limits are far beyond what you imagine them to be.

30

Suspend disbelief

You may be thinking "some of this sounds reasonable, but I don't know if I can buy into it totally." So don't. You don't have to believe everything I'm telling you, just temporarily suspend your disbelief. If it'll make it easier, don't believe anything for a awhile. Simply cultivate a mental readiness for *anything* to happen.

The scientist Albert Einstein wrote that there are "only two ways to live your life. One is as though nothing is a miracle. The other is as though everything is a miracle."

A quantum leap cannot happen if your mindset is flawed with skepticism and disbelief. Your doubts are not the product of accurate thinking, more of habitual thinking and mental junk. Concentrate your doubt on your own limits.

I can believe anything, provided it is incredible.

—Oscar Wilde

One way to suspend disbelief is to get a clear mental image of your goal. Imagine how it will feel, look and sound to be in the position you want to be. Most top athletes use such visualization instinctively to assure their top performance. Martial artists form clear images of their movements beforehand. As you view the results of achieving your goal repeatedly in your mind's eye, your brain will begin to accept this image, rather than your limited beliefs, as reality.

Embrace Change

One of the reasons I am asked to give motivational speeches for large corporations is that one major dilemma of modern business is to get people to blast out of their ruts, out of their comfort zone. Management wants their employees to take on the challenge of change, both to hone their skills in the face of competition and to move into

It's contrary to the law of nature for humanity to stand still. You either move forward or the eternal march will force you back.

—S.B. Fuller

higher levels of management. The best paid managers and employees of tomorrow will be those who embrace change.

People often fear change, assuming it will make things worse. Yet change is inevitable. It's also a chance to show your capabilities and strengths. Change forces you out of your comfort zone, your safe rut, and gives you a chance to learn and grow.

Life is like a mystery novel. Turn the page each day with an attitude of enthusiastic expectation. What will happen next? What will you find out about yourself that you didn't know before?

Leap Before You Look

Act. Make your move before you're ready. Don't get so wrapped up in preparation, research, and forming the perfect plan that you remain motionless. A person can make a career out of laying the groundwork. Getting ready is often nothing more than a stalling tactic. "I'm almost ready. I'll be ready next week. I'm working on it. I'm close." You're pulling a con game on yourself.

You don't need to know at the beginning how you're going to get there, but you need to know *where you want to go*. Rivet your mind's eye on the finish line. Visualize your arrival. Then *get started* and frame out the strategy and the details while in motion.

The ways and means will appear to you as you go, magnetized to you by the law of attraction. Solutions may come to you out of nowhere, so rapid fire that you barely have time to write them down. They will be simple, streamlined solutions to the problem.

Mobility is the crucial element. You'll discover you knew more than you thought you did. Once you set yourself in motion, you activate the *law of attraction*. You will magnetize the people and circumstances to you that will be needed upon arrival at your goal.

> *The shortest answer is doing.*
> —English proverb

A dream will only crystallize into reality if you pursue it. As you go after it, it becomes drawn to you. Pursuit shortens the distance between you and what you want. It alters the odds and becomes a dynamic exchange between you and the world.

You can think positive all you want, but what really gets the job done is positive action.

There is an element of shooting from the hip involved, but you're not operating wild or recklessly. You may have to tolerate some confusion, even a little chaos. You're going to shape your game plan as you go. Don't brood over potential problems and roadblocks. All you need for now is an aiming point and action.

Unwrap your gifts

We all have many gifts of talent and ability that we've never opened, usually because we're afraid. "I didn't need to know I was good at that!" It's an uncomfortable feeling, because now we're responsible for using the gift. What we call the gifted or high achievers are different in one important way. They accept their gifts. They accept and use their own talents and abilities and are not afraid of them.

Each of us has a unique "product" inside of us. Hiding inside you is a speech that only you can give, a book that only you can write, music that only you can play. If you die without opening your particular gift, you will have deprived me and the rest of the world of your unique contribution.

You may not have opened your gifts because they are so natural to you that you didn't even know they are there. Your destiny may actually mean doing something that you love to do and that comes easily to you.

A word of warning: opening your gifts can be a scary experience. What if you discover that you have more and greater talents than you suspected? It will be tempting to crawl back into your shell where you felt much more secure and comfortable coasting through life by modest means.

If you have a talent, it's your job to use it. God gave you talent for a reason, so bring it out and let the sun shine on it.

Everyone is gifted. All the gifts you need are inside you. The desires, the dreams, the curiosities that burn the hottest in your mind are the clues to where your gifts lie. Some informative questions to ask yourself: If I had only one year to live, what would I want to do for that year? What do I want my epitaph to say? Listen to your heart.

Seek failure

Thomas Edison, who patented over 1,000 new ideas in his life, experienced a great deal of trouble in his search for a new storage battery. A friend remarked on his lack of results after *fifty thousand* failed experiments. "Results?" replied Edison calmly. "Why, I have gotten a lot of results. I know fifty thousand things that won't work."

Everything looks like a failure in the middle of it. You can't bake a cake without making a mess in the kitchen.

Flops are a part of life's menu and I've never been a girl to miss out on any of the courses.
—Rosalind Russell

34

I always feared failure because I looked at it as a personal indictment. Failure is not an indication that you're not "meant" to have what you're going after, evidence that you should quit, or that you're not as good as you should be. It's merely evidence that you need more experience.

NBA superstar Michael Jordan stated on television that he had lost thousands of games in his career and taken 26 game-winning shots....and missed. His current success, he stated, is due to his ability to learn from failure.

Think of failure, problems, even pain as a positive sign. Failure is proof of growth and improvement. It is an absolute prerequisite for success because you can't succeed until you have failed so many times that you have learned everything you need to know. *Embrace* failure. It's a sign that you are getting that much closer to your goal because you will learn from failure what you need to do in order to succeed.

Quantum leaps are both exhilarating and terrifying. Perhaps, in some area of your life, you have already made one of these spontaneous leaps and know what I'm talking about. If you've never made a quantum leap, you will experience an astounding path to inner power.

Quantum leaps don't eliminate the need for hard work, but they are your reward at the end of all your effort, the sudden and seemingly effortless leap into a new state of being.

The Power of Attitude

*The last of the human freedoms is to choose
one's attitude in any given set of circumstances,
to choose one's own way.*

—Victor Frankl

What would it be like to wake up tomorrow morning with a different slant on life? Colors will sparkle with a new hue, food will have a slightly different flavor. Your angle of attack on the day's challenges will be just a little bit different.

One afternoon I was relaxing with my friend Reggie Jackson. I said, "Reggie you've hit 30 home runs or more several years in a row, a feat that very few other major leaguers have ever achieved. How did you do it?" He replied "Mack, it was easy. I've always felt destined to be great, destined to be good."

Can you imagine the power of that emotion, the power of that thought? That you feel destined to be great? No matter what happens, no matter how it starts out, that it's going to be part of a grand conspiracy to make you successful?

All winners create their outcomes in advance. Attitude is the fifth tenet of Taekwon-Do, which is *Indomitable Spirit*. It is the whisper of silent determination from within the soul that insures success. Science cannot define or explain the difference that attitude makes in any equation. It is the "x" factor, the wild card that creates a new outcome.

If you have ever closely observed a peak performer like Michael Jordan, you may have noticed: There are people who can jump higher than Michael Jordan. There are better shooters than Michael Jordan, better rebounders, better ball-handlers, simply stronger people in the league. Why is Michael Jordan so great? Simply because *he wants to be*. His attitude makes him better than the sum of his talents. He is the definitive and most important player on the team. Here's a simple equation that explains the abilities of peak performers like Michael Jordan.

$IA + AA \times A = PPP$

IA is inborn attributes, the talents that you're born with. Most of us are average in most things. We're average drivers, average cooks, average golfers. Yet everyone has at least one area of excellence in at least one area of their life. This is your inborn talent.

AA is acquired attributes, skills that result from training and practice. These skills are used to enhance and shine up your talent.

A is the wild card, the x factor: *Attitude*. Your attitude multiplies your talents and skills to create a synergistic result—an outcome that is greater than the sum of its parts.

The result is **PPP:** Permanent Peak Performance.

Attitude can make or break a business, a church, a home. There is no area of your life in which attitude is not critical.

Attitude is more important than facts

People are always confusing themselves with facts. "Here are the facts. Let's get the facts straight." Some of the facts are: I have two artificial hips, a plate and screws in my knee and two bullets in my right ankle. Considering the facts, I cannot run. Yet I kick over my head, do full splits, run, jump, and dunk a basketball. I defy the facts with my attitude and so can you.

Facts may be interesting, but they don't motivate you. Thomas Edison, who averaged a new invention every few *weeks* of his adult life, said that imagination is far more important than facts. Don't confuse yourself with facts—stay focused on what *you want*.

Attitude is more important than the past

What have you been told are the "facts" about yourself in the past? You're not athletic, you're not graceful, you're dumb, you don't have enough talent? These are not facts. They are someone's opinions, and they have programmed your mind for failure. Teachers regarded both Thomas Edison and Albert Einstein as slow learners when they were children. One teacher even went so far as to tell a young Albert: "Einstein, you will never amount to anything." What erroneous opinions of the past could be eroding your attitude right now?

Attitude is more important than education

Living in the streets of Chicago taught me that the world is full of educated derelicts. I ran into more than one person out there who had a college degree or Ph.D. We would sometimes fight for the same cardboard box.

If you are job searching, you will soon discover that top management companies care more about your attitude than they do grade averages or IQ scores. They have discovered that people with the right attitude can learn anything, and always get the job done.

Attitude is more important than money

It is more important than successes or failures. Attitude is more important than your appearance or talents. I have worked with countless professional athletes and students from every walk of life who achieved far beyond their inborn talents and skills because their attitude dominated their every action. With the right attitude, you simply don't accept "no" for an answer.

Just as a picture is drawn by an artist, surroundings are created by the activities of the mind.

—Buddha

Your attitude is the reason you will succeed or fail, whether you will relish life or just sit quietly at its sidelines. Have you ever known people for whom nothing ever goes right? They will tell you that the reason they are so unhappy is that life has been extraordinarily unfair to them. I have a relative who is an incredibly gifted athlete. He is 6'6" and when he was 13, he could throw a baseball at 92 miles per hour. Yet he is a mountain of unused potential, because he blames all his failures in life on the fact that he is black.

At a recent conference, I heard a wise and respected Native American elder called Grandpa Parish tell the audience: "All the words you hear today, yesterday and tomorrow—you don't need to remember all of them. Just find *one word* that will give meaning to all you hear."

I'm going to give you the one word that will give meaning to this chapter and to all of this book. Focus your full attention on the next paragraph. It is essential to your success.

Your *attitude* sets up a circle of invisible influence. It revolves around you and changes the facts. Quantum physics has already demonstrated how changing your *attitude* can alter the physical facts of reality. Just as the scientists saw change in the atom because they expected it, so do your *attitudes* result from your expectations, your beliefs about yourself and the world around you. Do you believe that you are deserving of good things to happen to you? Do you believe that eventually the events of your life are going to turn out well? Or do you feel life is out to get you and you don't really deserve to be happy?

The power of negative expectations is overwhelming. Negative attitudes may arise from what you were taught as a child. Simply the way your parents looked at you had a tremendous formative effect. Some parents bathe their children in loving looks. Others only look directly in their children's eyes when they are angry and shouting at them.

> *Man is what he believes.*
> —Chekhov

Have you ever met the eyes of a young tough or gang member and had them respond angrily "What are you looking at?" Whenever someone looks directly at them, they think they are being criticized because they have never known the power of loving looks.

In my research prior to the production of my self-defense tape for women, *I Will Fight Back*, I interviewed over 2,000 convicted assailants and rapists over a three year period. Almost 98% of prison inmates told me that one or both of their parents always told them they would end up in prison. They had managed to live down to their parents' expectations.

Parents who pass on positive expectations to their children, who tell them they believe in them and that they are special, have passed on a priceless legacy, a treasured heirloom. There is no greater gift you can give your children, your spouse, your loved ones, than your positive belief in them.

Even if you weren't given the gift of positive expectations early in life you now have the power to manufacture an attitude and keep it positive. If you find that you are creating negative expectations for yourself, study Chapter 13 on loving yourself. Some of the practices in that chapter can boost your self-esteem and create an attitude of positive expectations.

> *Nothing great was ever achieved without enthusiasm.*
> —Ralph Waldo Emerson

Your attitude is a choice. You can choose the attitude you wear every day just as you choose your clothing. You cannot change the past or other's opinions. I've discovered that my life is 10% the result of what happens to me, and 90% how I respond. You cannot control what the world or other people do, *you can only control your reaction*. You are capable of choosing your attitude at any moment.

Can you manufacture a great attitude, even if life is not going well for you? Try these methods to transform and maintain your attitude.

Treasure determination over speed

The race doesn't always go the fastest, it goes to the one who wants it the most, who says with passion and conviction *I want that*. The second year that I worked as a conditioning coach for the Oakland A's, Tony LaRussa came on board as manager. Professional sports can be a brutal world. When new management comes in, they often change all personnel. LaRussa fired me, sight unseen.

I loved my job, and I wanted it *bad*.

I called Tony and left a message. He didn't call back. I sent him a note at a meeting he was attending at a local hotel. I wanted to know why he fired me and a chance to meet face to face. He didn't answer the note. I called his room and he didn't return the call. So I went to the hotel and sent a bellboy into the meeting to see if he would talk to me. The answer was no.

So I walked into the meeting. All the coaches were sitting around a table having dinner. I walked up to Tony and said "Hello, Mr. LaRussa, my name is Mack Newton. I want to talk to you. All I need is two minutes of your time. If after two minutes you want to fire me, I'll leave." He reluctantly joined me underneath an olive tree on the side of the pool.

"Why have you fired me when you're not aware of the quality of my work?" I asked.

He replied, "First of all, I don't even believe in having a conditioning coach on my team. I've never had one and I've been quite successful."

> *If you refuse to accept anything but the best, you very often get it.*
>
> —W. Somerset Maugham

"That's true. I've followed your career. I watched you coach the White Sox in Chicago and I know you're a winner. You're a man who believes in success. You make changes, you're an innovator," I told him. "So am I. I've been a winner all my life. I've overcome a lot of stuff in my life and I'm going to overcome a lot more. You want people like me on your team. You need people like me on your team. You *want* me, you just don't know it yet. Don't make a mistake that you'll regret for a long time."

Tony thought about it for a long moment. "All right," he finally said, "I'll watch you work one time."

Everything hinged on that one chance. Winners love this type of challenge because it is a chance to shine. Losers fear such opportunities because they project failure and humiliation. My attitude was pumped to show Tony how good I really was. He rehired me and we spent the next eight years together and won three world Series rings. I still do consultation work with him.

Hang with the "right" crowd

Recently I noted that one student in my Taekwon-Do class could not seem to progress beyond the most basic level. Despite rigorous training three times a week, as well as listening to my lectures on philosophy and discipline, he continued with a lackluster attitude, his mind frequently wandering and injecting behaviors that would disrupt the class. As his instructor, I was at a loss as to what I should do differently to help him grow.

One evening after class, I found my answer. A group of teenagers standing outside my studio were verbally abusing and harassing people passing by. When I walked out to talk to them, they informed me that they were waiting for my problem student. There was my answer. His companions were dragging him down.

Like a sponge, you will unconsciously soak up the attitudes, behaviors and opinions of your closest associates. If you choose a negative reference group, that alone may be enough to condemn you to a lifetime of failure and underachievement. If you hang around with losers, you will become a loser.

If you want to have a positive, effective attitude, hang around with positive, loving, encouraging people. Consciously soak up their attitudes and behaviors.

Remind yourself daily that everything counts

There is no such thing as marking time, staying in one place. If you're not moving up, you're going down. Everything you do counts. Everything you eat counts, because it's making you stronger or weaker.

All your thoughts count; they are either making you a better or worse person. Nothing's neutral.

Do more than is necessary

If you are a salaried employee, work at your job as if it is your own business. What can you do to insure its success and your own position?

W. Clement Stone once told me that all true business leaders understand that 80% of their production comes from 20% of their workers. Those 20% are the ones that get paid well and are promoted through the ranks.

In your personal life, act as if the success or failure of your relationships is all riding on you.

> *Do your work with your whole heart and you will succeed — there's so little competition.*
> —Elbert Hubbard

Don't worry about what the other person is doing. What more can you do to insure the success and happiness of your personal relationships?

Be decisive

I once heard a pitching coach tell a player, "when you're going to throw a pitch, *decide* to throw that pitch. I would rather you throw an 85-mile-per-hour decisive fast ball than a 95 mile-per-hour indecisive fast ball."

Make a decision to be successful. Decisiveness shows in your body language and tone of voice. It strengthens your resolve and commits you to your goals.

You should only have to pull yourself out of a rut once. Never go back there again.

Act "as if"

You can practice attitudes for different occasions by acting "as if" you actually feel that way. The analogy I use with kids is this: Suppose you decide to climb an Arizona mountain trail? Are you going to go barefoot, or wear sandals? No, you're going to put on hiking boots because that's the only way to negotiate the rock and shale. If you go skiing, are you going to wear a tank top? Your attitude is the same as clothing in a closet. You can consciously choose the one you need for a given occasion.

Acting "as if" has a powerful effect on children in particular. Frequently parents bring their youngsters to my Taekwon-Do classes because they have no confidence or are being bullied at school. Long before they acquire the physical skills of self-defense, they learn to change their body language.

One boy named Dustin arrived in my class with extremely low self-esteem. His chin was always pointed at the ground and his classmates picked on him. Within two weeks, his mother was startled to learn that he was no longer bullied and now responded eagerly in school when the teacher called on him. The only difference? I had taught him to always walk with his head up and to play the "I Like Me" Game, a simple affirmation that you can learn in Chapter 13.

Sometimes you may need to change attitude in just a second or two, on demand. If my class is not going well, I need to change my attitude right away. Maybe this attitude of being nice and easy isn't working. I'll go to the closet and pick out one that's a little more stern. Or maybe I'm being too harsh and my students can't relate to me. I'll put on one that is a little more understanding. I change my attitude and act "as if" because that is always my choice. You are 100% in charge of your attitude at all times.

Follow your dreams

It's difficult to manufacture a winning attitude if you really don't enjoy what you're doing. Perhaps you won't admit to the fact that you don't really want that law degree that you're studying for. You really want to be an airline pilot, but you're afraid to admit it. If you spend your life doing something you really don't want to do, how can you ever be good at it?

Potential is something you are capable of doing but haven't done yet. Don't die with unfulfilled potential, with all of your best music unplayed, songs not sung, races not run.

Follow your own beliefs and faith

We are spiritual as well as mental beings. We have to have an attitude of faith, a spiritual basis for the things we want to do. In past years, I have had priests, rabbis and spiritual leaders tell me that they find no conflict between my program and their own faiths and religions.

It is to God's grace that you become everything you can be. When you fulfill your talents, I believe that you are performing on God's television. He enjoys watching you be all that you can be. When I do something particularly well, I look up and say "Did you like that? Was that good?" I have this vision of God being able to watch any scene on his TV and being tickled by the demonstration of our talents.

Yes!!! I knew you had it in you. I put it there!

47

5

Fear and Other Emotional Swamps

He who conquers himself is the mightiest warrior.
—Confucius

Negative emotions are the major barrier to maintaining a good attitude. Resentments, grudges, anger, self-pity, doubt, jealousy, guilt— they are like dragging around 300 pounds of excess luggage. You are making your life much harder than it has to be.

A temper explosion blocks the mind's ability to comprehend and learn. Wallowing in reactions to anger, resentment, fear or other negative emotions paralyzes the brain's messages to the body, so that energy is completely wasted.

The physical impact of the negative emotions cannot be underestimated. Athletes who are dominated by fear or anger will often lose their only chance at a championship.

At the root of all the negative emotions is fear.

49

Fear can shackle you in a thousand ways. It is a treacherous enemy that can paralyze you, steal your peace of mind and enslave you. Ralph Waldo Emerson said "We are afraid of truth, afraid of fortune, afraid of death, and afraid of each other."

Some of the more common fears are:

Fear of failure

Failure is inevitable when you are working towards your goals. The key is to think of failure not as a catastrophe, but as a stepping stone. One study showed that the average age of self-made millionaires in the U.S. is 54, with a history of *18 business failures* behind them. Failure is not a declaration proclaiming "You can't do this." It is a voice that says "You need to learn more." You don't fail, you simply produce results. When fear of failure strikes, read Chapters 6 and 8 to inspire yourself beyond fear.

Fear of loss

This fear can keep you imprisoned in an abusive relationship or a boring job. If you can't surmount this fear, you will live your life in a tiny cell of experience, never daring to discover what joys and challenges wait for you at the other side of that restricted world.

Fear of death

An old Arab story tells of a slave who borrowed a horse from his master because he had been dreaming about Death and was convinced that he could outrun it.

He rode for three days, to the point of exhaustion. On the third day, he faced seven trails from which he had to choose. He tried the trail to the north for a few hours, but doubt soon caused him to switch to a southern trail. Soon he switched again, and again, certain he was outwitting Death. After trying all six trails, he tried the seventh path where, 100 yards away, he was confronted by the glaring face of Death. "Where have you been so long?" asked Death, "I've been waiting for you."

The moral of the story is that you can spend your minutes, days and hours trying to avoid death or to make the most of your life while you're here. Death is unavoidable in the end, so why worry about it? Spend your precious time chasing your dreams.

> *Avoiding danger is no safer in the long run than outright exposure. The fearful are caught as often as the bold.*
>
> —Helen Keller

Fear of intimacy

This is a challenge for both men and women in our society. It's been said that it's much easier to get physically naked in front of some-one than it is to get emotionally naked. Tied to this is the *fear of rejection*. Will others love us if they know who we really are?

Read Chapters 13 and 14 on loving yourself and others. Not ev-eryone will like or love you, but if you have sufficient self-esteem, their rejection won't be such a blow. The reward is the possibility of truly knowing and loving another person who also loves you just as you are.

Facing Your Fear

Worry has been defined as an extended form of fear, based on indecision. Your imagination can create far greater horrors than real-ity. If you are steeped in worry, your thoughts can actually attract into your life the very things that *you do not want*.

Quantum physics and the law of attraction profoundly demonstrate how the state of your mind can affect your environment. In the Bible it says, "that which I have feared the most has befallen me."

How can you overcome fear? As has often been said, courage is not the absence of fear, it's the willingness to act *in spite of fear*. Emerson said "Do the thing you fear, and death of the fear is certain."

Gather courage to act in spite of your fears. The word *courage* comes from the Latin word *cor*, meaning "heart." Courage makes all the other virtues possible because you are creating a heartfelt challenge to fear.

> *Bravery is the capacity to perform properly even when scared half to death.*
> —Omar Bradley

All athletes have secret fears, and in my conditioning work it has been as important to deal with those fears as it is to assist their physical development.

Bo Jackson, who fans considered to be nearly invincible, was forced to face his inner fears when he came to work with me after his hip was replaced. Bo was afraid of no longer being Bo, of being the phenomenal powerhouse of energy, force and spirit that he had always been. And he had promised his mother, before she died, that he would come back and play major league baseball after his hip was replaced.

Recently I was sitting in my den, relaxing and studying the dozens of athlete's photos on the wall. The smiling, poised face of Bo Jackson leaped out at me. With the end of his career staring him in the face, Bo exhibited courage beyond belief. In severe pain, he committed himself to daily workouts of strength-building calisthenics, stretching, push-ups, crunches and specialized exercises to rebuild his hip muscles. It took nearly a year for him to get in good enough shape to play baseball with the Chicago White Sox, but he faced his fear of failure and pushed through.

He hit a home run in his first at-bat.

In addition to being a superb athlete, Bo is an incredibly powerful mental being. He understood the necessity of facing his fears down faster than I could teach it to him.

Bo is now even stronger in body, emotion and spirit than he was before the injury. Bo knows that, no matter what happens to him, he will always be Bo.

Anger

One of the most overwhelming of the negative emotions is anger. Anger has been called the great destroyer of happiness, perhaps the most destructive of all the emotions. Outbursts of anger can cause heart attacks, insomnia, strokes, broken blood vessels, migraine headaches, high blood pressure, skin outbreaks. It dumps fat into the blood and weakens the immune system. Rage has ruined marriages, relationships and careers. It destroys the developing personalities of growing children.

If anger were a disease, we would be spending millions of dollars trying to eradicate it. But it's not a disease, it's an innate part of the human psyche, with physical as well as emotional causes.

> *You will not be punished for your anger, you will be punished by your anger.*
> —Buddha

When you perceive that you are a victim of someone's aggression, your mind sends a danger signal along the pathways of the autonomic nervous system. The message is then relayed automatically to your adrenal-cortex, the part of your brain that prepares you for action. Your adrenal glands flood your bloodstream with adrenaline. Your body goes on red alert. *Alert-alert-alert — you are under attack.* Your blood pressure goes up, your respiration rate goes up and your whole body is ready to defend itself.

It's the ancient phenomenon known as *fight or flight.*

*For every minute
you are angry,
you lose
sixty seconds
of happiness.*
—Ralph Waldo Emerson

When I get angry, I not only can't think, I can barely see. I may want to hit or kick that person, to scream at them, to make them feel bad because I'm feeling bad. I may want to get even.

Retaliation in the midst of anger is unacceptable. You're also not fit to make a decision of any kind when mired in the fight or flight syndrome. Almost every decision I've ever made angry has been a bad one.

If you repeatedly have outbursts of temper, your self-control falters until you may have no resistance to this emotion. So you start getting angry faster at less and less provocation. You'll end up living a life of seething hostility and directing your anger at anyone and everything around you. Anger will become your automatic reaction to anything that appears to be a threat in your environment. We all know how fun those people are to be around, right?

If you've been conditioned to stifle your anger, as many women have been, then you will "keep a lid on it," by either denying its reality or boiling inside instead of striking out at the source of your anger. Your rage implodes until you are crushed under a burden of resentment, bitterness, and depression. Eventually you may become sick, because the internalized anger is like a slow poison dripping through your veins. Medical researchers call such people "Type C" because they are unable to express anger and seem to be significantly more prone to cancer.

Grudges and resentments also result from uncontrolled anger. Long-term anger causes you to become fixated on a person, problem or conflict. They are now taking up so much valuable space in your mind that you will lose the ability to think clearly. The situation will then manipulate you and your emotions because you are allowing someone else to push your buttons.

> *Jealousy and anger shorten life, and anxiety brings an old age too soon.*
> —Ecclesiastes 30:24

When I arrived in Vietnam, I was a very angry person. I hated my father to the point of obsession. I had a quick temper and could lash out unexpectedly with words or my fists at anyone who got in my way. Anger reared its head whenever I perceived that someone was taking advantage of me, causing me to feel like a victim, causing that internal pain.

Often anger is caused by frustrated expectations. It's a reaction when things don't work out the way you expected, or people don't do what you want them to do.

Sometimes I would even let people know in advance— "hey, you're starting to make me angry!" That set up my excuse in advance. I was warning them that if they continued to do whatever they were doing, my getting mad would no longer be under my control.

The fact of the matter is that *no one can make you angry.*

We have a tendency to blame other people and shift responsibility. We don't want to think we got mad on our own, rather that someone caused us to get angry.

You can see the extreme of this rationalization when men who abuse their wives or girlfriends say "I'm sorry, but you shouldn't have made me do it. You shouldn't have made me mad." What a cop-out! What a con game we play when we blame someone else for our reactions.

Anger is simply this: it is a response that you choose to a particular situation.

In every case, it's not the reality of what's going on, it's *your per-*

ception of what's going on that triggers the response. It is how you interpret this event to yourself.

You can decide to respond to difficulties in a calm, reasonable manner or you can respond with anger. You're always free to choose. It is not forced upon you.

Anger cannot be treated with a new medication, but with a new attitude, one which results from rooting out its basis in fear and eliminating it.

I don't agree with the pop psychologists that you have to express or get in touch with your anger. Medical research has shown that both explosions and implosions of anger are unhealthy for you.

You don't need to get in touch with your anger because anger is not the problem. It's the fear that is causing the anger.

Once you face and deal with your fears, the anger will dissipate.

Meanwhile, here's some practical suggestions for dealing with temper outbursts if you feel one eminent.

Pause to get your anger under control

I say to myself *stop being angry right now. Stop it this minute.*

Do whatever it takes, tell the person you will discuss it later and walk away from the situation, or count to ten, or take several deep breaths. Give yourself a mental time-out to get your anger under control.

Ask yourself if this is truly important to you

How much energy do you want to waste on everyday annoyances such as the person cutting in front of you in line or a spouse's crankiness?

If the matter is important to you, decide how you can effectively respond to the other person's hostility without exploding yourself.

Find a role model for patience

Get an image of someone you know who is very calm, and when you feel the first stirrings of anger, ask yourself how that person would deal with the situation. One of my role models is the greatest example of self-discipline and self-restraint— Jesus of Nazareth. He was abused, pelted with rocks and ridiculed, and in spite of all that was incredibly understanding and patient and forgiving. So I ask myself, how would Jesus respond?

Program yourself for patience

People aren't born patient, they're born as infants in a hurry to have their needs met, crying or screaming when they need something. A temper explosion is this same infantile need to demand what you want.

Patience is a growth process, made up of the little decisions you make every day.

I was a very angry person in my early adulthood and I used to get especially angry with children. They would frustrate me when I couldn't get a point across to them in class and I would yell and scream. Patience is critical with children, and I began to fear that if I didn't acquire it, I might actually harm or hit a child someday. I used visualizations of my role model for patience and pictured myself behaving the same way. I drew up a 3x5 card that affirmed "I am patient" and read it every day.

Programming myself for patience changed my life. I went from not being relate to children at all to having one of the top children's programs in the country. In 1983, I took a group of nine to twelve year old black belts to England for a demonstration before the Queen of England.

Don't rush to judgment

Stop judging people. When you're angry, you're always right aren't you? You are so right, that you have to tell the world that you are right in a very emphatic way.

Even if you are right, have you ever known anyone to agree with you just because you shout your opinion? An angry outburst will only put them on the defensive. When your boss or your spouse yells at you, do you think "Well, yes, their criticisms are correct and I'm going to have to work on that," or do you start thinking of ways to defend yourself and prove them wrong?

Withhold judgment for a little while to give yourself time to think, ask a few questions, and slow yourself down.

Agree with the object of your anger

A young child suggested this to me in a Taekwon-Do class when I asked him ways to avoid getting into arguments with people. Say to someone, "I agree with you on that point. Tell me more about it." Listen to what they have to say. If at the end of that, you're still not willing to agree, just simply drop it, walk away from it, let it go.

Use a straw man to make your point

People will accept your ideas much more readily if you tell them Benjamin Franklin said it first.

—David H. Comins

If you are arguing with someone in your family or an employee, and its important that you get the point across, I use this tactic.

"You know, I was reading a magazine last week and the person took this point of view....." or "I was listening to Walter Cronkite say on television....."

Let him argue against Walter Cronkite or

58

a third party instead of you. People, particularly if they are close to you, are far more likely to agree or at least change their opinion when the argument is with a third person rather than you. You will depersonalize the argument so it becomes a clash of opinions, not of wills.

Now you've got more of a discussion going on than a heated argument. Far, far more positive.

Repeat to yourself "I am responsible, I am responsible"

You are not responsible for the guy that cut you off in traffic or the business associate who insulted you, but you are responsible for the attitude that you choose to deal with the event.

Your self-esteem is a great defense against anger. As you learn how to treat yourself better throughout this book, you will be less likely to respond to others with hostility. When athletes, for example, have a high level of confidence in their own abilities, they are able to respond to a coach's criticism with a shrug and an apology rather than a sarcastic retort.

Letting Go

One path will carry you out of your fear and anger, and that is to accept what is and move forward. It's hard to let go of anger, because it means letting go of our sense of self-righteousness, of our self-justifications and most treasured grudges.

Unless you look beyond your anger and disappointment, you will continue to find yourself at the mercy of every negative force in your life. You cannot control what others have done to you. You can only control your own actions towards them.

I was always angry at my father because of his rejection, because he never said he loved me, because he always told me I wouldn't amount to anything. When I finally decided to let go of my anger towards my father, I mentally forgave every mean, cruel, vicious, spiteful thing he ever did to me and I've never mentioned it to him again.

Several years later I packaged up one of my most prized possessions—the championship ring from 1989, when I was conditioning coach for the Oakland A's and we beat the Giants by four straight games in the World Series.

I sent that $16,000 ring to my father as a symbol of my forgiveness. I decided he had done the best he could with who he was at the time. My father called me in tears after he got the ring. It's the first time I ever heard him say he was sorry.

Forgiveness was selfish. It freed me up from the guilt and allowed me to go ahead. It allowed me to become the person I am today and will be tomorrow.

If you want to progress, you must let go of every single grudge no matter how entitled you think you are to it. You must forgive them and you must go on.

> *Fear is the main source of superstition, and one of the main sources of cruelty. To conquer fear is the beginning of wisdom.*
> —Bertrand Russell

At the root of every negative emotion you will experience is fear.

Fear steals your peace of mind, your happiness.

Fear can create a total paralysis or mire you in a mediocre and bland life in which your limits are never tested, your boundaries never transgressed.

Facing your fears will automatically expand the walls that surround you.

60

Face your fear and move toward it

Use mountain top thinking to surmount fear. Don't look at what you have to do and how difficult it's going to be and all the obstacles you're going to have to overcome, because these thoughts will engender worry, fear and doubt.

Look to the mountain top. Project yourself forward to the achievement of your goals, to the place you truly want to be. What will it feel like, look like on the mountain top?

Don't worry about how tough it's going to be. This book will teach you what you need to know about forming goals, solving the obstacles and achieving your dreams. You are going to reach your goal. It is a foregone conclusion and it's only a matter of time.

> *You must do the thing you think you cannot do.*
> —Eleanor Roosevelt

Affirm with enthusiasm and conviction, "I can! I can do it!" Look to the mountain top and fear will soon begin to diminish and recede. It is a paper tiger in your path to power.

6
Stay Hungry

We act as though comfort and luxury
were the chief requirements of life,
when all that we need to make us happy
is something to be enthusiastic about.
—Charles Kingsley

Standing by my uncle's deathbed after I first came to America, I had my first inkling of what it is like to sacrifice your life to a meaningless goal. My father took me to see my Uncle Johnny, who was dying from emphysema. He was only in his thirties, but he looked ancient. His emaciated face was gray. He could barely talk as he coughed up blood and struggled to breathe.

I remember him saying that what he had always wanted most in life was to be a railroad engineer. Yet he had spent his whole life working in a post office because he had been told the post office can't fire you.

"Johnny get up!" I wanted to yell. "It's not too late. Even if you only drive a railroad car for five minutes, go out and do it now!" Of

63

course it was too late for Uncle Johnny. On his death bed he had only regrets for life spent in the secure but boring confines of the post office.

You must do what you want to do. Too often we drift through life without ever asking *Where am I going? What is my purpose here?* It's your job to chase your dreams. It's the only way you're going to be satisfied. It's the only way to feel fulfilled.

It's not the length of your life that really matters, it's the quality of your life.

Too often we quit just before the magic happens, whether it is with children, work or in life.

Many of life's failures are people who did not realize how close they were to success when they gave up.

—Thomas Edison

A fourteen-year-old named Chris Paul began training at my Chicago school. He was clumsy and not very good at the movements. I didn't think he had much chance of advancing. However, he loved Taekwon-Do with a passion.

"Mr. Newton, I'm going to keep training *forever*," he told me with a big grin on his face. He came early and stayed late for every class. He would repeat a movement *thousands* of times until he got it right.

Chris Paul became the first black belt in my class because he stuck with it long after others had dropped out. Soon things began to really click for him. He became an "overnight" success, winning the lightweight world championship twice.

He didn't quit before the magic happened.

You only need three conditions to overcome a crisis, whether it be professional, a personal relationship, parenting, overcoming an addiction or any other area of self-growth:

64

- You have to have a very specific goal. The goal must be written down with an outline of the steps that will get you there.

- You have to passionately *desire* that goal.

- You have to take action

Goals arise from your hunger, from your desire to follow your dream. A wish isn't good enough. Saying "I wish I had a better job" or "I'd like to lose some weight" is not a goal. Implicit in wishing is the suggestion that, although desirable, it will probably never happen.

Great minds have purposes, others have wishes.
—Washington Irving

Unless you write your goal down, it is not a goal. It is only a wish. There are three basic reasons why people choose not to set goals.

You don't understand the importance of goals

Analysts studied the Harvard graduating class of 1953, and found that only 3% had a clearly defined goal for their future. The study was followed up twenty years later and they found that those 3% were worth more in financial terms than the entire other 97% put together.

Without goals we walk around like a traveler without a map. The reason for goals is simple. Whatever you put your energy into will increase on its own. For example, have you ever had a toothache? The more you concentrate on it and worry the tooth with your tongue, the worse the pain gets. Then you may have been distracted by an engrossing conversation with a friend and briefly became unaware of the pain. Your mind and body will conform to the dominant thoughts in your conscious mind.

65

A goal gives you an aiming point, a new purpose on which to focus your attention. You will concentrate less and less on your dilemmas and failures, and more on the direction in which you're headed.

You're afraid that you will be laughed at or rejected

People become paralyzed by the thought of rejection. Have you ever confided a goal to your best friend or family member and heard them say "That's ridiculous. You could never do that." Almost every athlete has had the same experience. Someone told them they were too short, too fat, too skinny. It drags you down when you hear negative words from the person you thought would support you.

Others are intimidated by your goals, because they unconsciously know how powerful they are. If they think that you will move ahead or away from them, they'll try to talk you out of your goals. The solution to this is simple. Write down your goals and don't reveal them to anyone who is not also a habitual goal-setter themselves.

You are afraid that you will fail

You probably will. I have failed many times in almost everything I have attempted to do. I started a Taekwon-Do school in Chicago and it went broke. I started another one and it went broke. I have been out of business six times so far, totally broke. I failed because I was good at Taekwon-Do, but I still needed to learn how to run a business.

Today I have a successful studio and rehabilitative center that more than pays me a good living. I got so tired of going broke that I learned how to run a business. Failure is part of the success process. You've got to fail over and over until you learn the lessons that you need in order to succeed. Failure has taught me who I am and what I want to be. If you don't set goals because of a fear of failure, you are destined to fail anyway.

Failure never means that your goal is impossible. Believing that something is impossible is very dangerous, because your mind will bring that into reality. The "impossibility" becomes crystallized in fact. Break the word impossible into two parts:

I'm possible.

Coaches and athletes used to believe what they had always been told: that the human body is incapable of the speed required to run faster than a four minute mile. No one had ever broken that barrier until Roger Bannister made headlines around the world in 1954 by running it in 3.59.4 minutes. Since then, more than 700 professional athletes beat the four minute time and even lowered the record by another 15 seconds. Now even high school athletes have achieved it. Why was it not possible before 1954? Because people believed that it was not. One human mind surged forward and disproved the limits, and the feat became commonplace.

> *If one advances confidently in the direction of his dreams, and endeavors to live the life which he has imagined, he will meet with a success unexpected in common hours.*
> —Thoreau

Balance Your Goals

Balanced goal setting means that you acquire goals in three areas of your life:

1: Your family and personal life

2: Your career or professional life

3: Self-improvement

Many people only set goals in their professional life. Eventually their personal life suffers, their health suffers and finally their career itself suffers. Commitment to worthy goals requires balanced goal setting in all areas of your life.

Getting There

Not only do you need goals, you need the hunger to persevere until you get what you want.

Not many people know that the philosopher Socrates was a physically powerful man, a weight lifter in fact. One day a young student came to him and said "I want to acquire knowledge like you." Socrates said, "There are many opportunities to gain knowledge. Let me show you what it will take." He led the young man down to a nearby river and asked him to kneel down by its edge. Then he forced the man's face in the water and held him under with a powerful grip.

The youth struggled furiously, testing even Socrates' strength as he tried to raise his head. When Socrates finally released him, he asked the boy what he was thinking when his head was under water.

You have to want it bad. You can find geniuses on any skid row and average intellects as presidents of banks. It's what pushes you from inside.

—Charley Winner

"All I could think of," replied the youth, "was taking a breath. *I had to breathe air again*, there was no other thought in my mind."

"When you want knowledge as badly as breathing," said Socrates, "you will acquire all that you want."

How bad do you want your goals, your ideas, your dreams? People are always telling me "Well, I gave it my best shot but it just didn't work out." Your best shot may not be good enough. You must be willing to do more than your best, you must do *whatever it takes*. You must stay hungry enough to *want it* as badly as you want to live, to breathe.

Rarely are you called on to do whatever it takes, but you've got to be *prepared to do whatever it takes.* This willingness creates a form of invisible influence in your environment. It changes the facts of any situation. You magnetize yourself to your goals. It may sound like hocus-pocus, but I have seen it work countless times in my studio and rehab center.

Beverly Rubenstein, a grandmother with arthritis, bursitis and scoliosis, came to me in 1993 in a state of crisis. She had managed to alleviate pain with a program of diet and treadmill walking, but recently exercise had begun to aggravate her arthritis so severely that she was limping and in constant pain. Her doctor recommended hip replacement. After sobbing at a support group about the death of her youth and the need to accept her own deterioration, another woman told her about the rehabbing of athletes that I had been doing.

Reluctantly, she appeared at my door one morning. "I'm not sure if you want to work with a 62 year-old flabby Jewish lady," she said, "but I'm desperate and something inside me knows there's an answer to my problems. I've always dreamed that, as I matured, my body could regenerate instead of degenerate. I'm sick of aches and pains and a frumpy body."

I heard a great deal of negativity in her underlying beliefs about herself as she told me about an obese childhood, peaking at 235 pounds when she was 22 years old. The first time she attempted roller skating she broke her leg, and was discouraged from any further athleticism, never even learning to ride a bike, "I have poor balance and am very uncoordinated," she told me. Yet inside her was a hunger, a burning desire to master the challenges of aging with vigor and heart.

Today I can hardly recognize this remarkable woman. At age 65, she looks 50. She suffered no loss of mobility after the hip replacement and says that she is "in the best shape I've ever been in my life." She has slimmed down to a trim size eight, and has more flexibility and energy than some of the young people in my rehab classes. "I smashed my negative beliefs about myself," she recently said. "It's opened a whole new world of dreams, knowing that life's not over, that there are still accomplishments to come. I went for broke, and quadrupled my energy in quantum leaps."

> *Let me*
> *tell you*
> *the secret that has led*
> *to my goal.*
> *My strength lies solely*
> *in my tenacity.*
> —Louis Pasteur

Magical thinking will not produce a result. Beverly did not simply will her body to regenerate. She does whatever it takes, including long grueling hours of exercises that she had never believed within her capability. What do you want so bad that you are willing to do whatever it takes?

This hunger may require you to extend yourself into unfamiliar territory to learn something new, to find the one idea that will overcome failure. The martial artist Bruce Lee studied ballet to learn balance, as well as boxing and fencing to perfect his timing. Bo Jackson underwent a grueling physical rehabilitation to launch himself into a baseball career after a hip replacement made football impossible.

The only thing that guarantees failure in life is quitting. I'm never going to stop hungering and chasing after my dreams. My motivation to be my best springs from my love for my mother, who died when I was three months old. She was sixteen. She had a whole life of promise and potential before her, and yet she died after giving birth to me. My drive is for both of us. If her son's life means something, if I prove myself of some worth to the world, then her short life will have meaning as well.

Only you know what your goals should be and what will provide your motivation. In your innermost heart, what goals and dreams mean more to you than anything else? If you've only wished for them and quietly relegated them to some back corner, then it is time to bring them front and center. Be bold. Be OUTRAGEOUS. If you are overweight and have thought maybe you'd like to lose 10 pounds, decide to lose 30 pounds. If you are sick of your job as a banker and have always wanted to be a musician — do it. The writer William James gave us these three simple actions to change your life:

- Start immediately
- Do it flamboyantly
- No exceptions (no excuses)

I'll add a few actions of my own that might help out:

Think *past* the finish line

Martial artists do not break wood or bricks by concentrating on the breaking point, but thinking *through it* to the other side. See the final results of your goals and aim for them in your mind's eye.

Fall in love with your goals

You must care about something so deeply that it lights a fire inside and creates a magnificent obsession. Passion keeps you going when you hit the obstacles. The emotional heat must burn hot enough to protect you against the chilling effect of doubts and uncertainties, particularly the criticism that will come your way. Reaching your goals must be an act of love and faith, a passionate statement about how much you desire what you seek.

Visualize and dream to fuel your passion

Visualization is the ability to form a clear precise image of what you want in your mind and then hold that picture. See yourself as a person doing the things you want to do, having the things you want to have, accomplishing your goals. Your brain doesn't know the difference between actual experience and the one you visualize. So when you visualize, you are teaching your subconscious mind that you can do it.

The ice-skater Dorothy Hammill used visualization to create her flawless and graceful performances. When she prepared for competition, she took her music and a fan into the center of the ice. The fan was to create the sensation of wind rushing against her, as it did during every performance. Sitting on the ice, with the wind blowing across her body and her music playing, she would mentally start her routine and perform every motion in her mind. She would do every jump perfectly, land it perfectly, cut the ice evenly and smooth. When it came to performing, her subconscious mind already knew exactly what to expect. She never exhibited hesitation as she approached a difficult move, and has become known for her effortless, perfect performances.

I teach professional athletes to visualize themselves performing certain ways in certain situations. I call it the quick sports programming technique. When you have visualized an action beforehand, your mind will recognize the situation and your body will respond automatically, before you even consciously have time to react.

Rely on unseen and universal forces

You don't have to do this all by yourself. Unseen forces are phantom powers which can't be fully explained. I've plugged into it many times and been able to touch the physical manifestations of this type of assistance. It was like magic. I've seen results come out of nowhere, with no logical explanation for the results that occur.

These unseen forces seem to operate through your unconscious mind. You might be hit by a flash of inspiration while you're sitting alone. A creative solution may come to you in a dream. You're so overwhelmed by the solution to a problem, that you leap up immediately and write it down.

The universe is inherently creative. All the energy of every person, every plant, every creature that has ever lived is still here. Some people call it the oversoul or the world soul. "The mission of the universe is to seek out all possibilities, be copious, giving all things equal opportunity to 'do their thing,'" says the physicist Fred Alan Wolf.

You don't have to understand what this power is, you only have to accept and use it. I can't see electrical energy and have no clue as to how it works, but I'm very familiar with its uses and its power.

> *You can have anything you want*
> *if*
> *you want it*
> *desperately enough.*
> *You must want it with*
> *an inner exuberance*
> *that erupts*
> *through the skin*
> *and joins*
> *the energy*
> *that created*
> *the world.*
> —Sheila Graham

Allow possibilities to materialize. Your willingness to make the quantum leap is the enabler. It's a little like playing bridge. You can't see your partner's cards, but you're bidding based on the power of their hand as well as yours. The unseen forces will come to your support. Count on it.

Trust in the power of pursuit

Have you ever dreamed about getting something, or wanted something so strongly that it consumed your thinking? Dreams begin to crystallize into reality when you pursue them. Think about it. Almost everything that you have right now in your life, you've had to *go after*. Pursuit requires action. You can think positive all you want, but what really gets the job done is positive action.

Pursuit shortens the distance between you and what you want. It alters the odds. It becomes a dynamic exchange between you and the world. By the law of attraction, that which you desire will be drawn towards you.

Erase the phrase "I'll try" from your vocabulary

When you say *I'll try*, you are excusing failure in advance. Replace it with *I'm doing it* or, if it's a goal that's not immediately in your grasp, say *I'm learning to do it*. If all you're going to do is try, you don't really want it bad enough to make it worth the effort.

Commit ideas and goals to paper

This will provide evidence to your mind that they are "real." A fleeting inspiration that is not written down will probably be lost tomorrow.

No whining. No excuses

Your mind can be incredibly creative at coming up with excuses. "I've had a hard day at work." "My kids made me so angry I can't see straight." No one else's actions or attitudes should be used as an excuse for not pursuing your goal.

There's no such thing as giving too much of yourself to your dream. Sing like you don't need the money. Love like you'll never get hurt. Dance like nobody's watching. It has to come from the heart if you want it to work.

74

7

Quantum Learning

Life is full and overflowing with the new.
But it is necessary to empty out the old
to make room for the new to enter.

—Eileen Caddy

Can you imagine a school with a curriculum so powerful that it could teach you to overcome any crisis, face any challenge, solve any problem? Such a school exists, and it's right inside your head. If you haven't mastered its guidance, it's because you haven't yet learned *how to learn* through the process of *active learning*. Active learning does not mean memorizing facts, as you may have done in high school or grade school. Active learning is absorbing new information, then drawing new connections, and gaining the *understanding* that leads to wisdom and creativity, not merely knowledge.

Here's a surprising fact: your brain has the same physiological capacity as Albert Einstein or Thomas Edison. Yet despite the fact that we all have similar brain functions, neurologically speaking, some have managed to develop their thinking capacity to a very advanced state by active learning. Your brain has billions of nerve cells, called neurons. As you actively learn, these neurons interact with each other along branches called dendrites. These branches can form a vast web in the brain which transmits old and new knowledge, old and new ideas.

Knowledge comes by eyes always open and working hard, and there is no knowledge that is not power.

— Jeremy Taylor

Research has shown that the greater number of these branches that exist in a person's brain, the less susceptible they are to the effects of dementia and Alzheimer's as they age. It's the same principle as your physical body: *use it or lose it.*

Active learning also makes creativity possible, because you are clearing a pathway for new connections in the brain. Creativity is not limited to artists, writers and musicians. We are all inherently creative — a combination of being curious, experimental, playful, intuitive.

Creativity just means finding a solution to a problem that makes life a little more pleasant. If you have ever been trapped in some situation from which there seemed no way out, and yet you found a way, you were behaving creatively. Creativity is a new insight into a problem or situation.

How do you engage in active learning? This chapter will give you several simple but profoundly powerful paths to wisdom and creativity.

Empty your cup

In the martial arts we have an important concept: the usefulness of the cup is in its emptiness. If I want to drink a glass of tea from a cup that has already been filled with sand, that cup is totally useless to me. The only way to use the cup is to empty it first, so there is room for something more.

A well-known Zen story demonstrates this principle. A student came to a master for instruction. The master invited him to join him for a cup of tea. The student bragged about the abilities he had acquired so far, how much knowledge he had of the martial arts and its movements.

The master began to pour the tea, and continued pouring until the cup overflowed into the saucer and the young man's lap. The young man leaped to his feet. "What are you doing?" he yelled. "The cup won't hold anymore."

"Like this cup," replied the master, "your mind is so full of judgments, opinions and speculations that there is no room left for me to teach you. Until you can empty your mind, I will not be able to instruct you."

Jesus taught a similar principle in the Sermon on the Mount. Jesus informed his followers "Blessed are the meek, for they shall inherit the earth." Some scholars believe that a truer translation of the word meek is *teachable*. Those who can welcome new knowledge will inherit the future.

To empty your cup means to learn without preconceptions, without assuming you already know it all. *Oh, I've been there before. Been there, done that.* That's the trendy saying.

I've seen the results of keeping a "full cup" many times. Teachers and coaches see it when they need to teach the same people the same principles over a long period of time.

Tony LaRussa would face the exact same team every season and have to get them ready to perform again at a high level. He had to say the same things to them. Some players said "I've already heard this," turned off and missed the point. In my classes, there are students who have been with me for four or five years and have heard the principles in my talks many times, yet they can still get new information if they don't approach it with the attitude of "I know that already."

Have you ever wondered why a young child will want to listen to the same story over and over? Their minds have not yet been corrupted by a school's demand to memorize facts. They are actively learning by emptying their cup to hear new meanings, new mythology, new symbolism every time they hear the story.

No story is the same to us after a lapse of time; or rather, we who read it are no longer the same interpreters.

—George Eliot

You may have experienced the same thing as an adult. Have you ever seen a movie for the first time and it was so good that you talk a friend into going with you so you can see it a second time? In watching it again, you'll see things you didn't see the first time. Some movies may take three or four times to understand completely even though you know the general theme.

Emptying your cup in order to learn does not decrease your confidence in what you have already learned or experienced. It simply makes room for something new to enter. The business writer Dale Dauten says that "Confidence is when you have something to teach; arrogance is the belief you have nothing to learn." The arrogance of a full cup will keep you from expanding and growing in your inner power. If you are still alive, you still have something to learn.

When I approach a situation that I'm even slightly familiar with, I try to study it as if I'm seeing it for the first time. I listen to speakers and take notes as if I've never heard a presentation before. I listen between the lines because I want to go at it with an empty cup. I learn more from my students than they learn from me, because I'm not presuming I already know all that I need to know.

With each new experience or new thought, or old experience and old thought, empty your cup and you will learn more than you ever thought possible.

You can learn things today that you weren't capable of recognizing yesterday, or last month or last year, because you are at a new and different level of development and growth. *So are the people to whom you're listening.* They may well have new knowledge to impart to you, if you don't tune them out because you think you've heard it all already.

There are many ways in which you can "empty your cup," to learn without preconceptions of the truth.

> *Education is the ability to listen to almost anything without losing your temper or your self-confidence.*
>
> —Robert Frost

Ask questions

Ask questions of someone in a field you know nothing about, or read a book about something in which you have no knowledge.

Take a second look

Read or see for the second time a book or movie that you enjoyed during your teens or early twenties. What new information do you find from your perspective now?

What if you can't fail?

Ask yourself what you would like to learn if there was *no possibility of failure?* The purest and most advanced learning took place in your childhood when you had no concept of failure. Your mind was a sponge. You learned the complicated mind and muscle coordination required to walk and run. Numerous falls did not deter you. You learned at least one language and were capable of learning several if they were

79

spoken to you. In a few short years, you began to read and write, learning about 90% of the words that you would use in your lifetime. You were encouraged in these endeavors by your parents, because no one presumed you would fail. The learning ceased when others taught you the possibility of failure. *"You can't do that, you're too little. You're not fast enough to play on the team."*

Eliminate the negative

Did you have a teacher or a parent who called you stupid or clumsy or worthless when you were a child? If your cup is already half-full of negative self-images, you will be unable to fill it with new ideas. Negative projections are not only useless, but inaccurate information. Empty those voices out of your head right now. Use positive affirmations to reassure yourself you are capable of making quantum leaps in your learning. Read again the chapters on *The Quantum Leap* and *The Power of Attitude* whenever necessary to bolster your sense of a positive outcome.

Play

Search for new information like a child at play. Make it a game. Have fun. What would you do if nothing were riding on the outcome? When I was a kid, I was sometimes restricted to the back porch. I wasn't allowed to leave the area and I had no toys or TV with which to amuse myself. With a child's natural tendency to play, I began the "mind games" that would benefit me in later life. I would sit for hours and create images out of tree patterns and clouds. Dirt and rocks and twigs and sticks became playthings. I would take a twig and break it and make

Without this playing with fantasy, no creative work has ever yet come to birth.
—Carl Jung

80

it look like a horse's head. A broken white patch became a horse's mouth and I stripped bark down to fashion a mane. I literally created a horse, which I then could ride. Creating my own little world was good practice for my work in rehabilitation. I can still work instead my head, calling upon a skill that is just like magic, solving problems as if they were childhood games.

Make a paradigm shift

Look at problems with a different set of assumptions. This is much the same as the paradoxical thinking required to make a quantum leap. Try being illogical. What is the exact opposite of conventional thinking in the matter you are considering? If you are trying to climb a wall, check first to see if there is a window or door you can slip through. If you're pushing against a river, try going with the flow instead. Look for new solutions, new information. Overcome the addiction to your old methods.

One doctor told me that the only way he could understand how I rehabilitated his patients was to remove himself from his medical training, which was very narrow. "I also have to drop my attachment to conventional approaches," he said. "Then I can see why you're getting the success you're getting."

Just listen

Startle your spouse or partner the next time you have an argument with them. Shut up and just listen. Pretend you have never heard his or her opinions before. In conversations with our significant other we tend to think that we're very, very right, and so we often tune out and simply continue expressing our own viewpoint. Listen like you've never heard it before and you may hear something different.

Act "as if"

If you find it difficult to listen to a dull or dry speaker, act *as if* you are really interested. Use positive body language, such as leaning forward and focusing on the person's face rather than sitting back with arms crossed and eyes wandering. Listen between the lines. Take notes like you've never heard this information before. If you make the person to whom you are listening think that what they are saying has value, you may actually inspire them to more interesting ideas.

Listening as an art form

The best managers and salespeople are listeners. Some, however, think their greatest ability is the "gift of gab." They spend so much time talking that they never discover their customers' and employees' needs. When I worked in sales with a medical supply company in Illinois, I learned to listen well. You're more effective when your client or prospect decide for themselves what they want to buy.

If you listen long enough and find out what they want, they'll convince themselves of what they want to buy. It's the easiest way in the world to make a sale.

> *There is no such thing as a worthless conversation, providing you know what to listen for. And questions are the breath of life for a conversation.*
>
> —James Nathan Miller

Listening is an art. It's *paying attention.* When you listen intently to another person, you are saying "I value what you are saying. I value you." You will be amazed at how much new knowledge you can acquire when you learn the art of active and attentive listening. Once you have developed listening to an art form, you'll find that you actually enjoy listening more than you enjoy talking.

You'll find out so much more about

yourself and the person to whom you're listening, that you'll almost feel you're meeting that person for the first time.

It's been said that since we have two eyes and two ears and only one mouth, we should use them in that proportion. Watch more, listen more, and speak less.

Try these ways of becoming an artist at listening and learning.

Adjust your position

Face the other person directly, don't sit askew or sprawl. Lean slightly toward the speaker. If you're standing up, shift your weight slightly forward. Watch their eyes and mouth. Don't let your eyes wander. When you adjust your body language to make it appear that you are fully engrossed in the conversation, you will find that your mind just naturally follows.

Listen without interruption

Most listeners are just waiting for a pause so they can interject their own thoughts on the subject. If you are busy thinking about your response, you aren't really listening to the other person.

Listen quietly and calmly

Listen patiently. Act as if there is nothing else in the world that you would rather be doing than listening to what this person is saying. Listen for as long as it takes for that person to say it.

Pause

Pause 3 to 4 seconds before you say anything in reply. This is not only a very classy thing to do, you also give the information a moment to sink in. You avoid interrupting the other person, who may be only pausing to catch their breath or gather their thoughts. A pause is powerful, because you make clear with your silence that you consider what they have said to be of value.

Ask questions

Develop questions that clarify what they are saying and insure that you fully understand their message. There's an old saying "errant assumptions lie at the root of every failure." When your knowledge fails you, it is because you have assumed things to be true that aren't.

Eliminate errant assumptions by asking open questions such as "How do you mean that?" As a listener, you should accept 100% of the responsibility for making sure you understand what is being said.

When you are the speaker, you should also accept 100% of the responsibility for the other person understanding you. These two simple efforts would eliminate virtually all communication problems.

Ask open-ended questions, which cannot be answered with a yes or no. A verse from Rudyard Kipling demonstrates this idea:

I have six honest serving men
They taught me all I knew
Their names are what and why and when,
and how and where and who.

Use these six questions to expand the conversation and your understanding:

- ◆ *What* was the situation?
- ◆ *Why* do you think it happened?
- ◆ *When* exactly did it occur?
- ◆ *How* did this take place?
- ◆ *Where* did it take place?
- ◆ *Who* was with you?

Feed back the person's words to them by paraphrasing. Not only are you giving the speaker a compliment, you are verifying that you actually understand what has been said. When another person finishes speaking, pause for three or four seconds and then say, "Let me be sure I understand you. The way I understand what you're saying is this....." Then feed it back in your own words. You will build a tremendous ability to communicate. Until you can feed a person's words back to them correctly, you haven't really learned what the person is saying.

Write it down

Take notes during a speech, meeting or even in an important conversation with one other individual. The average person speaks between 150 to 200 words per minute. However, you can listen at 400 to 500 words per minute. That means that one-third of the time I am talking to you, you are thinking about something else, because your brain can process words faster than I can speak.

Note-taking is valuable because it slows your mind down to the speed at which the person is talking. You will slow down and retain more of what is being said.

Employ genuine listening

Act as a sounding board to help another person understand themselves and resolve their own problem. Don't assume the other person has a small concern which you can solve briskly and then hurry on your way.

Listen sincerely and patiently, observing their body language at the same time. It's a higher form of active listening, adding simple reflection. Don't add personal opinions.

Therapists use this way of listening to rephrase the person's words and send them back to them in a different form. Not only does that person understand the problem better but may gain some insight into the solution.

For example, if a friend sits slumped in front of you and delivers a litany of complaints about her boss, you might respond "You sound as if you are feeling overwhelmed with the way things are going at work." You are not only reporting back her words, but reflecting what appears to be an underlying theme. You're helping her dig for a deeper meaning.

A student of mine had a much younger brother in one of my Taekwon-Do classes. One day he came up to me after class and said "I really hate my brother." Before I understood genuine listening, I probably would have chided him with something like "Oh, you don't really hate your brother, you just think you do." Instead, I reflected and responded "It seems to me that you feel that I'm paying too much attention to your little brother, and not enough to you."

The boy broke into tears. "I don't think you love me anymore," he sobbed. "Even my parents seem like they love him more than they love me." The young man didn't hate his brother, he simply needed reassurance that his parents and teachers still loved him.

The art of communication goes far beyond just hearing words. If you listen attentively and actively, with an empty cup, you will soon discover your mental and creative abilities expanding in quantum leaps.

8

What's Important Now?

Every moment is enormous and it is all we have.
−Natalie Goldberg

Do you ever find yourself sitting at your desk at work, gazing out the window, wishing you were somewhere else? Have you ever thought "Things will get better when I'm married," or "when I'm making more money," or "when I get to take a vacation?" Or does your mind drift to what you could have had "if only" you hadn't broken up with your spouse or the boss hadn't nixed your promotion?

Ralph Waldo Emerson said we become what we think about all day long. If you are focusing on past failures or mistakes, you're going to become angry and fearful. Holding grudges is a sure sign you are living in the past. You are bringing up something which has already happened and cannot be corrected. Probably 40% of what we worry about has already happened and can't be changed. Yet we give it a lot of mental space every day. Frequently our minds drift back to the past, even if it's as recent as a day ago.

If you're worrying about what the future's going to bring, you've created anxiety and stress. You begin to think with your "monkey mind."

Thoughts collide against each other. You start wondering what you'll have for dinner tonight, what that noise under the hood means, and if the boss will like today's presentation, rather than what is happening *right now.*

To cure future worries, ask yourself what outcome you seek for the future. Since the future is largely determined by what you do in the present, you must focus on what you do right now to establish the future you desire.

Mindfulness, focusing on what's going on *right now,* keeps you in touch, awake and attuned to the rhythms of your life. As it says in the Bible, "Sufficient unto the day are the cares thereof."

Capture the moment, whoever you are. None of us is here forever.
—Adrian

Often our attention is split by the demands and activities of daily life, leaving us operating in a semiconscious state. Have you ever had a driver make a sudden lane change in front of you without looking? How often have you gone for a walk or drive with no conscious memory afterwards of what you saw? If your body proceeds through the day like a robot, while your mind is elsewhere, you have lost countless opportunities for growth, for creativity, and for discovery. You must be *present* to succeed. That means being "in the now." That's really the only time you have. Whatever you are thinking right now, that's where you are.

Being in the present means quieting the endless jabbering of the mind, allowing life to flow forth rather than forcing events. You may have had this kind of experience while engrossed in writing or reading, making love, or being in the zone described by athletes, or a state of flow as described by artists. When you are in that divine state of awareness, past and future recede and the present moment is full of magic.

Taekwon-Do has given me and my students a lesson in performing in the present. Taekwon-Do requires total focus in the moment. Incredible power can be packed into one movement, as you have seen when one strike breaks boards or bricks. It requires intense concentration on one task to the exclusion of everything else going on in life at that moment.

In a Taekwon-Do match, as in any sport, intense concentration on the present creates an acute state of sensory awareness. Not only are your own movements more fluid and controlled, but you are often able to anticipate your opponent's moves. The speed of competition leaves little time for reflection or a wandering mind.

> *Never lose a chance: it doesn't come every day.*
> —George Bernard Shaw

Frequently, books and speakers propose you get into the "now" through meditation. That is not the subject of this chapter. Meditation is a passive state. So is positive thinking, positive expectations, visualization, the power of attraction. These are all true and valid, but in the end, your success in life is going to depend on what you *do*. No matter how positive your attitude, there is still only one way to succeed, and that is in an active mode. The acronym WIN stands for *do* **W**hat's **I**mportant **N**ow.

Ask yourself what you should be doing right now. *If I want to be a good father or mother, what should I do right now?....If I want to close that sale tomorrow, what should I do right now?....If I want to remain healthy in my eighties, what should I do right now?*

I've always espoused a philosophy of short term pain for long term gain. You will often see teenagers or very immature adults going for the short term gain—quitting school, buying a new car instead of

89

Real generosity toward the future lies in giving all to the present.
—Albert Camus

saving, drinking and partying rather than studying. Bite the bullet early. Do what needs to be done now so you can reap the rewards and enjoy the rest of your life.

You must be present in an active mode to win. That applies to relationships, life and sports and everything else. When you're thinking *and* doing positively, you've got it all working together. Positive thinking alone will not work. Commit yourself completely to action.

When you find yourself drifting to the past or the future, try these four ways to ground yourself in the present:

Ask yourself one question

Ask *What is the most important thing for me to do right now?* Don't ask what do you "want to do" or even necessarily what others "expect" you to do. What's the *most important thing* for me to do *right now*? Keep asking that question until you find an answer that requires action in the present.

A friend recently broke up with his girlfriend. He's in pain and living in the past. "I miss her so much, that's all I think about," he told me. I asked him what he thought was so important that he should be doing it right now? "I guess I've got to forget about her and move on," he said reluctantly. Since that is still a negative thought rather than a positive action, I asked him again: "Having said that, what's the most important thing for you to do?"

"Meet other people."

"What's the most important thing for you to do in order to meet other people?"

"Get out and do things!" he replied emphatically. By going out and meeting new people, he was at least acting in a way that would prevent a lonely tomorrow. He is now living in the present preparing for a happy future.

What if it's the future that is causing you anxiety? Let's turn my friend's worry around. He just broke up and he's worried that he's going to be alone forever.

"What's the outcome that you seek?" he should ask himself.

"I want to have a family, I want to have a partner."

"What's the most important thing you need to do to make that happen?"

The answer to worry and anxiety is purposeful action. Focus on the outcome you seek rather than sitting around thinking you'll be lonely forever. Anxiety and worry are arguing for your limitations, mentally arguing for what you *don't want to happen.*

Always ask yourself, *what's the most important thing for me to do now?* Write down an answer to the question, if it helps, and keep on asking the question until you come up with a positive action that can be taken *now.*

> *It is not impossibilities which fill us with the deepest despair, but possibilities which we have failed to realize.*
> —Robert Mallet

Silence the inner critic

The inner critic is that little voice in the back of your mind that passes judgment on every action you take. *How could I be so stupid?...I always say the wrong thing...I'm so clumsy.*

Phil Jackson, coach of the Chicago Bulls, says in his book *Sacred Hoops* that professional athletes go through the same mental process. "Everything they've done since junior high school has been dissected, analyzed, measured, and thrown back in their faces by their coaches, and, in many cases, the media. By the time they reach the pros, the

91

inner critic rules. With the precision of a cuckoo clock, he crops up whenever they make a mistake. How *did that guy beat me? Where did that shot come from? What a stupid pass!"* The inner critic drains vital energy from all your actions, and sabotages optimism and positive thinking. There are several ways that, with practice, will silence the inner critic.

Identify the critic's voice

The first step is to become aware that the critic is sabotaging you. Recognize the negative self-talk that is undermining you. Write down the inner monologues in your head and identify them as positive or negative voices. Do you find your self-talk peppered with words like *can't* or *never* or negative self-images such as *stupid, worthless, clumsy*?

Change your focus

Challenge the critic with positive affirmations. *I am learning and growing...I am smarter today than yesterday.* Respond automatically to bad experiences with a positive assertion: *That was unpleasant, but it's not the end of the world. I've learned something so that I can do things differently next time.*

Enjoy the moment

Focus on the sights, sounds and activities of the present moment. Perhaps you will discover something you haven't noticed before, because your mind was always elsewhere. Taste the sweetness of fruit. Feel your muscles when you exercise or stretch. Experience the air across your face as you run. Study every expression on your loved one's face as she sits across the dinner table. Listen to the birds outside your window. When you develop the ability to savor present moments, you will have the *power of presence.* You will be more effective on the job, in your relationships, and all your activities.

Adjust your body language

Acting *as if* can change your attitude and physical chemistry. Stand erect, breathe deeper and keep your chin up. If you slump with downcast eyes, you are easier prey for the inner critic.

Affirm the moment

Use affirmations to dispel the clouds of worry and obligation. Remind yourself at numerous points during the day *I'm here now*, or *I'm in the present.*

Separate problems and facts

Knowing how to deal with difficulty in the present moment requires understanding the difference between facts and problems. *Facts* are the reality of your world to which you must adjust, while *problems* are subject to change by your actions.

If you're out riding a bike, for example, the wind speed and the heat of the sun are facts. You cannot change them, you can only decide how to adjust to their presence, by how fast you pedal or the clothing you wear. What to do about the hill you're approaching, however, is a problem. The hill is amenable to hard work and pedaling, just as the problems in our lives are amenable to our intellect. You can conquer the hill but you can't conquer the wind or the sun, so you have to work that into your view of how you're going to ride. The wind is blowing or it is not, it is raining or it is not. We have to accept facts and work them into our world.

One of the most useful ways to deal with any difficulty in life is to ask yourself these questions. *Is it a problem?* If so, you can apply your intelligence to finding a solution. *Is it a fact?* If so, the smartest thing to do is just accept it and incorporate its presence into your world view.

It's also helpful to refer to problems as challenges or situations.

Calling it a situation don't seem quite so threatening as calling it a problem. Situations you can deal with, challenges you can rise to.

When the present moment is unbearable

Sometimes the present moment stinks. You are in pain and you're just sick and tired of how you're feeling. It is hard to fight on when it hurts. I completely understand people who accept their limitations rather than try to surmount them. People often think I am so strong that I never falter. They don't know that I could give up in a heartbeat. I was often in intense pain in the years leading up to two hip replacements, and again during my recovery. I often wondered why I was doing it and if I would ever be as good as I once was, or if I would ever be out of pain.

Students in my rehab classes suffer the same type of pain. Sometimes they want desperately to give up, particularly when they realize that they don't know how soon they will overcome their pain, or even *if* they will. Sometimes when my students feel they just can't push any farther, I tell them "Go ahead and give up right now if you want to. Go home and change your focus, read or watch TV or just sit. Give up. It'll make you feel better. Just come back tomorrow." I have mentally given up lots of times. Then I came back the next day, refreshed and ready to return to the present moment's problems.

Give up for a day, if you must. Just don't give up your entire life.

You know what is important in your own life now. You have the answer in your mind. Don't be intimidated by your own genius and your own possibilities.

What's the most important thing for you to do now?

9

Cooperate with Life

There are joys which long to be ours.
—Henry Ward Beecher

How do you cooperate with life when it frequently seems to be at odds with you? Have you ever heard some disaster-prone individual complain "If I didn't have bad luck, I'd have no luck at all"? Paranoid people have the feeling that lurking around every corner is a new danger waiting to pounce. Friends never arrive on time, loans don't come through, supplies are not here, they get the flu right before an important meeting. The world is out to do them in, so they naturally expect the worst out of every situation.

Inverse paranoia is a phrase coined by business executive W. Clement Stone, who believed that no matter how difficult a situation first appears, it is actually part of a universal plan, a conspiracy, to make you a great success.

What an astounding difference such an attitude will have: *to believe that no matter what happens, the universe has entered into partnership with you to make you successful.*

That shift in attitude alters everything: your expectations, how you talk to other people, your mindset, your aura, your outlook, your approach, what actions you take, all are transformed based on that mindset.

One writer once described a flat tire he got on the way to the airport. Cursing and disheveled from the inconvenience, he missed his flight and would not be able to attend an important meeting. He later learned that his flight had crashed and all aboard had lost their lives. He began referring to the incident as his "spiritual flat tire" and transformed his attitude towards life's little adversities.

The recent best-seller by James Hillman, *The Soul's Code*, proposes that each soul has a destiny to which it is called. Each of us, he says, tries to answer the fundamental question of our lives: "What is it, in my heart, that I must do, be, and have? And why?"

Hillman believes that each soul has a guardian that assists him in finding the answer. Plato and the Greeks called this spirit a "daimon," the Christians "guardian angel," and in modern terms we might call it our heart.

Whatever name you call this guidance, it waits for you to begin realizing your goals, your destiny, your dreams. It is like the "invisible forces" I described in an earlier chapter. For me it remains nameless, but I experience its genius and support over and over in my life and the lives of my clients and students.

One must never, for whatever reason, turn his back on life.
—Eleanor Roosevelt

If you cooperate with the life you have been given, you will find that it will support, encourage and inspire you. Life not only wants you to realize your destiny, it will conspire with you to do so.

96

What are some ways you can cooperate with rather than battle life?

Be easy on yourself

A golfer practices his game alone one sunny afternoon. As he tees off on the 18th hole, he slices the ball and it sails down the fairway, takes a right turn and flies off the course.

Since he's by himself, he gets another ball, tees it up, takes another swing and hits it down the fairway and plays out. As he reaches down to pick up his ball from the final hole, he sees a bunch of people running down the fairway towards him. He can tell by their body language that they're pretty mad.

"Are you the guy that hit this ball off the fairway?"

"Yes I am, but that's okay. I have plenty more balls. You can keep it."

"That's not the problem. When you hit the ball off the fairway, it went through the windshield of a car. The driver lost control, went off the road, ran into a tree and knocked it down, blocking the path of a fleet of fire engines. A whole tract of homes burned to the ground. What are you going to do about it?"

He thought about it for a moment, then replied. "I'm going to turn my grip a little more to the left."

The golfer is not going to punish himself with guilt. He is simply going to find a new approach that will eliminate the problem in the future.

Be easy on yourself. Don't attack yourself or call yourself names, saying things like *I never say the right thing. I always do the wrong thing.* Punishment does not work as a motivator for either children or adults.

Not only does punishment damage your sense of self-esteem, you are also setting yourself up to do the same thing again. You are reinforcing behavior that is already in place, but you haven't done anything to help you perform differently in the future. When faced with the same circumstances in the future, you're bound to repeat the same action.

If your computer stops working, do you grab a club and smash it a couple of times? You're not going to make it work, you're just going to destroy whatever is left of it. Beating yourself over the head for perceived failures has the same effect.

I used to be an expert at fighting life. When something went wrong, it was somebody else's fault or it was because I was too short, too tall, not good looking enough. I often called myself stupid and engaged in all sorts of self-punishment. I was in an adversarial relationship with myself.

If you walk out of the office after you've made a sales call, and remember that you didn't include a key element or you forgot to take advantage of a close, do you say *Why do I always miss those opportunities? I'll never be any good as a salesman.* That's punishment. You are fighting life.

Is life not a hundred times too short for us to stifle ourselves?
—Nietzsche

Develop the ability to be your own best friend, to cooperate with your own life, to be easy on yourself. Just change your grip.

When something goes wrong, immediately decide what you will do the next time you face that situation. How will you respond the next time you feel pressured by a time demand or someone shouts at you? You can say to yourself, *Okay, I didn't like what I did or the outcome, so the next time I'm in that situation, I'm going to do it differently.* That's being easy on yourself and setting yourself up for change.

Life is going to bring that next time to you, so forgive yourself immediately. You can do a better job. It's part of the learning process.

Give Up Guilt

One frequent form of self-punishment is guilt. You decide to "do your time" with self-induced guilt before you forgive yourself. Guilt is a cesspool of emotion that prevents you from making any realistic changes. Guilt restricts and shrinks your life. Soon you'll begin hiding out from any event or circumstances that will cause you to mess up again.

Riddled with guilt, your life will eventually become a very narrow band of experiences with a very narrow band of people. Life becomes predictable, mundane and boring because you are avoiding anything and anyone who might cause you to become mired in guilt and self-punishment again.

> *Guilt*
> *is*
> *the Mafia*
> *of the mind.*
> —Bob Mandel

Instead of thinking how badly you've screwed up, think about what you need to do to change. Give yourself verbal instructions. *The next time I begin to get angry, I'm going to slow down. I'll breathe deeply and count to ten.* Or *I will just stop, shut up and listen.*

Don't be sorry—be better

I used to find myself constantly apologizing to people for my actions or behavior, whenever I felt that I had offended someone. It took me years to learn a simple solution: *Don't be sorry. Be better.* Being able to say "I'm sorry" may alleviate your conscience, but it doesn't alter the damage you've done, and it doesn't excuse the need for change.

Use Kipling's advice again to invoke change. Ask yourself six specific questions:

- *What* am I going to do?
- *When* am I going to do it?
- *How* am I going to do it?
- *Why* am I going to change?
- *Who* are the people I will make this change with?
- *Where* am I going to make this change?

Learn to be patient

Your life may change in a heartbeat or it may take many months or years. Don't project the future or get hung up in thinking it's going to happen right away. It will happen. Success is predictable. I am standing here as an example of that. It's been a long road from my near-death in Vietnam to my success as an instructor, speaker and businessman today. The process becomes joyful, exciting and immensely fulfilling when I cooperate with the life that was given to me.

A good and wholesome thing is a little harmless fun in this world; it tones a body up and keeps him human and prevents him from souring.
—Mark Twain

Smile at adversity

Adversity can help you because it gives you just the tools you need to be successful. Goals have obstacles built in, so expect adversity. Don't go around them, go right through them. If feelings of failure begin to cast a cloud of doom around you, reread the chapters on *Stay Hungry* and *The Power of Attitude.* You are always capable of changing your attitude, just as you select a clean set of clothes to wear every morning.

A Chinese proverb says that a man without a smile should never open a shop. Attitudes are contagious. A bright smile or laugh will attract far more positive people and events into your life than a deep frown. And it's easier. It takes 13 facial muscles to smile and 111 muscles to frown.

Quit Complaining

Henry Ford said it well: "Never complain and never explain." Complaining undermines both the speaker and the listener. Have you ever slipped into a one-upmanship game of complaining with someone else? *Isn't it appalling what so-and-so did? Isn't it awful that prices are so high? Isn't it terrible weather? Isn't it dreadful that business is so bad?*

Life will reflect back to you whatever you are expending. It's the law of attraction and concentration, which states that whatever you dwell upon is attracted to you and grows in quantity. Or, as the Bible says, "As you sow, so shall you reap." The habit of finding things to complain about attracts other complainers to you. The more you complain, the more you will find to complain about and people to complain to.

Real men and women never complain. When they have a problem and there's something they can do about it, they take action.

People often tell me their problems. My usual response is: "You are faced with a real dilemma. What are you going to do about it?"

You can always tell the difference between the losers and the winners. Losers finger-point and assign blame. Winners recognize that it doesn't matter now how we got a hole in the boat, it matters how we get it plugged.

Do you recognize yourself in any of the following responses?

101

Losers	Winners
• *Whose fault was it?*	• *What can I do about it?*
• *This will never work.*	• *We can do this.*
• *Why doesn't somebody do something?*	• *Here's how I'll solve the problem.*
• *It's not my fault!*	• *I was wrong but now I can fix it.*
• *I'll never amount to anything.*	• *I'm good at this now, but I can get better*

Fake it till you make it

Acting *as if* creates a reality. When you *act* positive, enthusiastic, powerful and optimistic you'll start to feel that way inside.

Smile even when you don't feel like it. Soon the exercise of those muscles will cause your attitude to become more warm and sincere. Even if you don't believe that the universe is in partnership with you, *act as if it is*. Look at the events of your life as if they are clues. What was my partner planning for me? Did anything good come of this? Is there any way I can create a positive outcome?

All the basic laws and principles that I talk about intertwine and overlap. Laws of attraction, of reciprocity, of concentration and cooperation, all touch each other. Subtle differences in behavior can bring about tremendous results.

10

What Experts Don't Know and Doctors Can't Tell You

I confess that in 1901, I said to my brother Orville that man would not fly for fifty years... Ever since, I have distrusted myself and avoided all predictions."

—Wilbur Wright

Do you feel intimidated by experts? From M.D.'s to mechanics, we often feel obliged to listen to the experts when they tell us what to do, even when it flies in the face of our own common sense.

And yet experts have been making fools of themselves for quite some time. Teachers informed Albert Einstein's parents that their child was mentally slow, lazy, and "would never amount to a thing." Even the genius Einstein erred when he pronounced that "there is not the slightest indication that nuclear energy will be obtainable."

An eminent doctor back east wrote me a letter when I started working with Bo Jackson. He told me I was making a fool of myself. "People cannot play professional baseball with an artificial hip," he told me. "Mack, I have been replacing hips for 15 years. I know *for a fact* that an artificial hip cannot stand the stress of running, sliding and swinging a bat."

I told him "Doctor, I fully appreciate your knowledge and your experience, but there are obviously a few things about the human spirit that you know nothing about. The one thing you are not considering in this equation is his attitude."

Bo Jackson had what was a powerful motivator—he wanted to do it for his mother. There was no doubt in his mind that it *could be done*, because I had already rehabilitated my artificial hip and played baseball in simulated games with the Oakland A's. I was the conditioning coach for the team, so I had to play every position to know what effect it would have on their bodies. Most observers didn't even know I had an artificial hip. I had also rehabbed several other student's hips in between, so there was no doubt that Bo could do it.

Experts can be intimidating because they sound so very sure of themselves. Experts often quote "facts" to you, based on their experience and knowledge.

However, these facts may in reality be only problems that are amenable to your effort and intelligence. How do you tell the difference?

Stocks have reached what looks like a permanently high plateau.
—Professor of economics, Yale University, 1929

Everything that can be invented has been invented.
—Commissioner of US Office of Patents, 1899

I think there is a world market for maybe five computers.
—Chairman of IBM, 1943

If, for example, you have a spinal cord injury which confines you to a wheelchair, every doctor, scientist, and exercise coach would probably agree that you will not be able to use exercise, positive thinking or any other means to get out of that wheelchair and run.

In that case, you are probably best accepting your disability as a fact and employing every means you can find to stay active and healthy despite that fact. Many wheelchair athletes have developed tremendous upper body strength with tennis, chair racing, and other sports. The scientist Stephen Hawking lives in a body that is racked with Lou Gehrig's disease and can no longer move even a single muscle of his body, yet he continues to develop his inner genius in books and lectures. I have tremendous respect for the people I know in wheelchairs that continue to live their lives with vigor and power despite the facts of their injuries.

You are a potent triple play of mind, body and spirit, assisted by unseen forces. You can accept and adapt to *facts*, as well as conquering *problems* as they emerge.

You may find it difficult, however, to always know whether a situation is a fact or a problem. The experts have achieved their status by a lifetime of experience and learning and knowledge. Should you defy them?

There are some guidelines for assessing the fallibility of doctors and experts, but first let me tell you a story about a woman who defied all the "experts," even me, and proved that her injury was not a fact, but a surmountable problem.

Mary Hook, a slim, attractive woman in her early fifties, had her hip replaced as a result of injuries from a fall. Soon her days were filled with pain. She loved to travel, garden, and play with her grandkids, but the agony prevented most activities. A doctor advised her to do water aerobics, which helped when she was in the water, but pain resumed as soon as she crawled out of the pool.

She was referred to an orthopedic surgeon who informed her that the artificial hip stem had loosened. They would have to revise the hip, which meant another full scale hip replacement. Mary didn't want surgery because she knew there was no guarantee that the new hip would be any better than the one which had already been causing her so much pain.

She heard about my work through a mutual friend, Neil Lomax, who at the time was a quarterback for the Arizona Cardinals and had rehabilitated his hip in my studio. Mary came to see me and said she immediately trusted me because I didn't make any claims or promises. In fact, I was doubtful that I could help her. An artificial hip is a mechanical device, and I knew of no form of exercise or rehabbing that would cause bone to regrow around the stem once it had loosened.

I sent Mary's x-rays to three doctors whose opinion I respected and who I knew to be very conscientious. The verdict came back the same from each one. There was no way to tighten a loose hip by any means other than surgery. I regretfully told Mary that I would be unable to help her.

"But you can," she insisted. "I just know it."

"I've never done anything like that, and neither has medical science," I replied. "I don't think it's possible."

"Please help me. I want you to do it. I know you can do it."

I wanted to help her so badly because Mary is such a sincere and pleasant person. I thought about it for a week.

This was an example of a student taking a quantum leap for herself, without my encouragement and despite my doubt and caution. I had to reframe my thinking and take a similar mental leap to get onto her plane. Finally a plan came to me out of the blue. It was wild, it was improbable, but it was the only possibility.

Mary worked hard every day at the exercises and strenuous stretching that I had devised. She was so exhausted and sore when she left the studio that she would just go home and tumble into bed. After four months of this, she was still in pain. I was beginning to feel very guilty, because she was paying me to make her better and she believed in me, but there was no sign of improvement. I hinted that perhaps it was time to quit, but she would have none of it.

Mary asked me once how the process worked. "Will I know when it has happened?" I told her that she would know when there was no longer any pain.

Not long after that, I put her on the stationary bicycle and asked how her leg felt that day. She replied "it feels great." She paused and broke into a smile. "I can't remember the last time it hurt."

Mary Hook made medical history, because her x-rays now show the hip is not loose. Doctors can't explain it, because they have never seen it before, but they agree she no longer needs surgery.

Mary's story demonstrates one important principle: Your belief can literally move mountains, if you back it up with effort and hard work. She wanted it so badly that the universe cooperated with her and allowed the full rehabilitation of her hip.

If you have a similar burning belief in a possibility, then you should never let the "experts" talk you out of it. You are the ultimate authority on *you* and what you can accomplish.

But what if your mind is filled with doubt? Despite expert advice, you are still not sure if you are dealing with a problem or fact. Ask yourself several important questions before you decide to defy the experts:

Do I know myself and my body well enough to make this decision?

You must be in tune with your body to understand it. Only people who have challenged their bodies, understand, respect and accept their bodies are experts. You have to first of all know your body and have some experience. A woman who has had three pregnancies is going to be much more aware of problems or danger signals than her husband or even her male doctor.

I've exercised so much that when I sprain an ankle, I know if it's going to be better the next morning or whether I better go to the doctor and get it x-rayed. If you haven't experienced the subtle differences in pain, you may think a hurt is a hurt is a hurt. All hurts feel different to the one who has experience with their body.

If you have little experience or appreciation of your body, you must take the word of a doctor. This is how we have given the doctors the power that they have. They didn't really ask for power over our lives, we gave it to them. Many of them don't even want it. They want us to accept the responsibility for our own health and well-being and to use them as a tool.

Have I asked for more than one expert opinion?

A couple of years ago, I began to experience pain in my jaw and neck when exercising. A year ago I found myself straining to breathe during a 42 mile bicycle training ride and was unable to finish. I went to see a doctor, who smiled at my concern. "You're just getting older and you can't exercise as hard as you did when you were younger without getting out of breath. Don't worry about it."

I've lived with this body for 52 years and I know the difference between being out of breath and not being able to breathe. I had never experienced this particular sensation and so I knew he was wrong.

Another doctor I consulted listened in depth to my symptoms and ran tests. He discovered that I had a valve deficiency, brought on by untreated childhood rheumatic fever. My aortic valve had calcified and I was now pumping blood during strenuous exercise through a main artery which had not grown since childhood. The only reason I hadn't keeled over by the age of 35 was because of the strength of my heart and lungs and lack of cholesterol in my arteries. Blood pressure, an athlete's conditioning and pulse rate otherwise indicated a healthy heart.

The valve was replaced in 1997 and I'm now fully recovered and back to my normal level of activity. If I hadn't searched for another opinion, you would not be reading this book. Instead you would have read about the exercise fanatic who dropped dead of a heart attack in the middle of a workout.

Have I educated myself?

Ultimately you are the only authority on you. A doctor will willingly or reluctantly accept control over your health, but you're still left with 100% of the results.

How do you educate yourself? Talk to everyone you can find who knows something, read everything you can find in the library or on the Internet, discuss it with people who have been in a similar situation.

When I first began studying artificial hips, doctors told me I would have to be over 50 or 60 before I could get one. Doctors still sometimes advise patients to wait as long as they can stand it before replacement. It sounds as if the doctor is thinking of your welfare, but in reality they are stealing your life. Will you have any quality of life if you can't walk or run, dance or play tennis?

I wrote to doctors in Phoenix, Chicago and California for more information. Extensive reading about arthritis and what it was and how it could be treated led me to the Hospital for Special Surgery in Manhattan which works exclusively with joints and has done a lot of work with what they call CAPS, Computer Assisted Prosthesis Selection. They had a biomechanical engineer and a number of doctors on staff, and specialized in the working of joints.

Combining their knowledge with the knowledge I had already gained of the body's motion through the martial arts, I was able to help change doctor's opinions about when joints should be replaced. The rehabilitation that is now possible helps those with arthritis, even some as young as their twenties. Doctors now give artificial joints to children who are born with deformities, let them grow with it and replace it when they need another one.

Always search for a doctor who will listen to you and one who is interested in your opinion. The doctor does not know more about you than you do. Doctors didn't study *you* in medical school. They studied plastic and cadavers and machines and equipment.

The real you is spiritual and mental, how you see, feel and sense. You are the best person to make a decision about your health, as long as you are willing to take responsibility and educate yourself.

Has anyone else accomplished this goal?

If they haven't, that doesn't mean that you shouldn't go ahead and be a trailblazer if you believe strongly enough in the possibility and are willing to back it up with undying effort. History is full of firsts.

However, if you find that someone else has already accomplished your particular goal, now you know who the real experts are. Ask them for advice and guidance, which you can apply to your own particular situation.

Lou Adler, the general manager of a Phoenix business, had already quit mountain climbing and training horses due to severe arthritis in his shoulders, hands, back and knees. After back and neck surgery to repair fused disks, his doctor told him to spend at least five hours a day lying flat on the floor.

After arthroscopic surgery on both knees, he was told that within a few years both knees would have to be replaced. He had a friend with an artificial hip who had been rehabilitated at my studio and decided to try the same route they had.

"Mack knows what to do because he's been there," says Lou. "I'm doing stuff at 66 that I couldn't do at age 46." Although he still has some discomfort from arthritis, he has regained his full range of motion. He now rides his mountain bike ten miles a day over rough terrain, using all 21 gears with no trace of pain. He's lost over 70 pounds, and has transformed himself into a fit and trim man who has taken full responsibility for his well-being and health.

> *An expert is someone who knows some of the worst mistakes that can be made in his subject and how to avoid them.*
> —Werner Heisenberg

Am I only believing what I want to believe?

Are you just trying to find a doctor who's going to tell you what you want to hear? Wishful thinking cannot enter into your decisions. As I've said before, positive thinking alone will not change your situation.

I once had a young man come to me on crutches, referred by a local chiropractic doctor. He could no longer work due to back injuries from an auto accident. After I started rehabbing him, he went to an orthopedic surgeon who told him "You're moving in the right direction. If you continue with these exercises, you'll probably be fine in

111

three or four months."

Workouts were long and hard and that was not what this man wanted to hear. He consulted another surgeon who said "I can do microscopic surgery on your back and you'll be back to work in a week."

"You can always invest another month or two in exercise," I told him. "If you don't get better, you can still have surgery. However, if you get cut now, you may not be able to come back and do it through exercise." Surgery on or near the spine always contains risks.

He chose to believe the one doctor, however, over the advice of myself and two other doctors, and went under the knife. He has not walked since. He came back to the studio, but there was nothing I could do because now he had a serious neurological problem that wasn't going to respond to exercise.

To make the best decision, consider the medical profession's dictate: *First, do no harm.* We live in a society that suggests that there is a pill to swallow or a painless method of getting what we want. The easy path contains a number of potholes and dangers. Don't hand over control of your life to the doctors or the experts because you want an easy answer.

When you've got two conflicting opinions, you're always better choosing the method that will give you the most control. You may need surgery. You may need to research it to the point at which you're able to say "yes, this is what I need." Don't forfeit control. You are the expert.

11

Women and Power

We are not interested in the possibilities of defeat.
—Queen Victoria

Women often have mixed feelings about power. In movies, television and books, powerful women tend to be represented as lacking femininity, even cold and calculating. Powerful men are presented as warriors and heroes, rescuing the gentle, victimized woman, who is being slapped around, stalked, assaulted, threatened.

Yet any woman, despite her age, size or appearance, is capable of incredible strength and power in one critical area of her life.

Place yourself in the following situation: As you turn on to your street coming home from work, you know immediately that something is wrong. Fire trucks and police cars are scattered all over the block. You pull up to your driveway and see flames leaping out of the windows. The baby-sitter is standing safely outside but your three year old daughter is still in there. You jump out of the car and run towards the house. The only thought in your head is saving that little girl. The neighbor tries to hold you back for your own safety. Can he stop you?

Can two firemen stop you? Does it matter if they are six-foot muscled men and you are five-foot-two? If you are determined to get to your child, no physical force will stop you. This was demonstrated by the famous story of a woman in Detroit who single-handedly lifted a car that was crushing her child.

Consider another scenario. You're working in your back yard garden while your daughter is napping. You hear her cry out, and run in to find an adult male sexually assaulting your child. Is there any doubt that you would stop him? Would it matter if he had a gun?

When I asked a group of executives what they would do in this situation, several women shouted without hesitation "I would kill him." Whenever I pose this scenario to women, they are vocal and vociferous in declaring their anger and commitment to defend their daughter.

Then I ask them one more question. "Would you fight as hard for yourself?"

Silence. I am met with blank stares as they become emotionally speechless.

Why wouldn't you fight as hard for yourself?

Caring women will fight valiantly and passionately for their children, their family, even their country or their company, but often not truly for themselves. I call it the "responsibility gap." Just as you assume responsibility for your child's welfare, you need to assume competency and effectiveness for your own sake.

The raging power that will defend your child against harm can be harnessed in your own self-defense as well. At the heart of the matter is the need to recognize that you are valuable and essential to life, simply because you are you.

Here are four little words that can change your life: *I will fight back.*

Having been raised by women, and spending over twenty years training women in Taekwon-Do and self-defense, I know the power, ferocity and capability of women. I have watched very feminine, very attractive women become intense fighters.

While teaching self-defense to the Chicago police department, I saw a battered and bruised woman come into the station. I was riveted by her swollen and bloodied face in a very personal manner, because she looked like my great-grandmother, who had raised me. That's when I began developing a self-defense program for women which is now called "I Will Fight Back." In preparation, I interviewed over 2,000 incarcerated criminals and talked to over 860 women that were victims of violent crime.

The need for change bulldozed a road down the center of my mind.
—Maya Angelou

In the process, I discovered a great deal about a woman's thinking in relation to her own defense. Someone always goes to jail after battering or raping a woman, and unfortunately, it's usually the woman herself. She becomes a prisoner of fear. Women live in a world that men don't even begin to understand. You've had to live your life, take care of your children, work your jobs, while living with the kind of fear that makes you afraid to go out alone running or jogging, or to the store at night alone. "How can a woman ever achieve peace of mind?" I asked myself.

To make it worse, women often blame themselves for violence. In my experience, every woman blames herself in some way for an assault or rape. *I must have given him the wrong signals, I must have led him on, I shouldn't have made him so angry, why didn't I see this coming?* Feelings of guilt and fear result in a frightening statistic: *Less than 10% of rapes are ever reported.*

Recent crime surveys show that over 1800 women are raped per day in the U.S. Nearly one-third of rapes happen to children between 11 and 17 years old. As many as one in five adult women will be raped at some point in their lives.

Even if you never go out in public alone, or carry Mace or pepper spray, you are far from safe. More than 80% of rape victims know their attackers, which means that you are in far more danger from a spouse, relative or acquaintance than you are from a man jumping out from behind the bushes.

In the years spent teaching women self-defense, I learned something critical: physical techniques are easy. You can learn the physical ability to defend yourself in a few short hours in any self-defense course. You are far more capable that you suspect, even if you are short, frail or in a wheelchair. The most demanding part is understanding and employing the emotional and spiritual characteristics it takes for a woman to fight back.

There is more than one definition of rape, according to the dictionary. Rape is:

- The crime of forcing another person to submit to sexual intercourse.

- The act of carrying off or abduction

- Abusive or improper treatment—violation.

Does that last definition of rape surprise you a little?

Rape of your spirit does not only occur when someone kidnaps you in their car. It can happen when you are belittled or sexually propositioned by your boss, when you are slapped or punched by your husband or boyfriend. It can happen when you are standing in line at the store or in an elevator and the man behind you stands too close. You can feel his breath on your neck. You know his brushing touch wasn't accidental.

Let me tell you something about the criminal mind. The abusive man does not expect you to fight back. He is depending on your fear of making a scene, or of unjustly accusing an innocent man. The man in the elevator who "accidentally" touched you does not expect you to whirl around with fire in your eyes and say "Back up, mister. You're playing me too close." A woman who believes in her own ability to fight for herself has an advantage over a man that has nothing to do with muscular strength. If he knows that she knows how to fight back, he would never touch her. Men know there's nothing more dangerous than a woman with a bad attitude.

> *Remember, no one can make you feel inferior without your consent.*
> —Eleanor Roosevelt

Have you ever gotten so angry at a husband or boyfriend that you screamed *NO—STOP THAT!* right in his face? Perhaps you saw a flash of fear in his eyes. When you saw that momentary look in his eyes, you probably felt guilty and apologized immediately.

Abusive and violent men depend on several very noble aspects of the female character:

- You are generally more trusting than a man, or at the very least you are unwilling to make a harsh judgment about someone else's motives.

- You are capable of great empathy and compassion.

- You would rather find a solution to a problem by talking and negotiation rather than an aggressive or violent action.

117

These characteristics decrease the likelihood of your responding to violation with instant ferocity and the man knows it. Psychologically, most men are frightened of women who are willing to fight, to stand up for themselves.

Law enforcement officials used to have difficulty in training women officers in their readiness to use a lethal weapon. Sometimes a woman would actually be shot with her own gun because a criminal could take the weapon away from her.

We must change in order to survive.
—Pearl Bailey

Trainers countered the problem by appealing to another of a woman's basic instincts: protection of loved ones. "What will happen if this man gets past you?" they asked. "If he can take your gun away from you, where will he go next? Will he assault or murder an innocent child? An elderly woman? You are their last line of defense."

This training is valuable and made its point. However, I would add one very vital reason to fight back with all the power that is in you: *You* are worth fighting for simply because you are you. *I will fight back* is part of a mental philosophy that begins in your heart and is carried out in your mind. Why should you be a victim? Why should you deprive the world and your children and your loved ones of all the uniqueness and beauty that is you?

This spirit of fight is part of the spirit of life. If you will fight back when a man tries to overpower you, you will also fight back when life overpowers you, by injury, cancer, illness, loss and fear.

Fighting back with warrior-like strength of conviction does not preclude your femininity: You can still be caring, nurturing and loving to your spouse, family and friends. You are ready and willing, however, to instantly stand up for yourself when attacked or threatened.

118

Know the warning signals.

Men who are excessively jealous and possessive, drink heavily or use drugs, who try to make women feel guilty for refusing their overtures, have aggressive body language, and have an obvious dislike and disrespect for women are more prone to rape or abuse of women.

In your goal to fight back, there are several self-concepts that you must address in order to fully realize your power:

What is your self-ideal?

Your self-ideal is a composite image, a bundle of beliefs about an "ideal woman" that you have borrowed from church, parents, family, and from what you admire about other people. What ideal of yourself do you have as a parent, a wife, a driver, a businesswoman? Do you have an ideal of yourself as a fighter?

> *What one has to do, usually can be done.*
> —Eleanor Roosevelt

The psychology of becoming says you're constantly traveling in the direction of your ideals, your dominant thoughts.

What is your ideal self?

What is your self-image?

Look in your internal mirror and ask how you see yourself on a mental level.

Everything you do, you have already prepared for in advance with this image. If you panic, it's because you have already seen yourself as a panicky, helpless person on the mental level. If you fight back, it is because you see yourself as a fighter.

Whatever your self-image, it may not be consistent with the way other people see you.

119

Do you have self-esteem?

How much you like yourself is the core of your being, your personality. Everything you do or accomplish will be a direct result of how much you like yourself. Liking yourself feeds your self-esteem and self-concept.

Liking yourself is the primary motivation for fighting for yourself. You must be totally committed to yourself and your life.

Traditional Taekwon-Do practice as well as self-defense courses can have a potent effect on the confidence and self-liking of women who undertake its rigors. Judy, an attractive, slender 23-year-old, recently achieved the status of blue belt after a year's work. She confessed that she had been terrified when she came to the first class. "I wasn't in shape," she said, "I couldn't do a single push-up or crunch. Everyone else seemed to know what they were doing. But my boss thought the training was so valuable that he had offered to pay for his employee's classes, and so I thought I would at least try."

Judy attended classes faithfully and stuck with it, gaining strength and self-assurance each month. Unknown to me, she was in an abusive relationship at the time.

"He was destroying me," she said later. "My self-esteem was being ripped to shreds, but I loved him." She had an epiphany in class one day.

" Here in Taekwon-Do I had become a self-confident woman. I had discovered I could do so much more than I thought I was capable of. But my outer life no longer matched my inner life."

She immediately showed her subversive boyfriend the door, and finds herself in charge of her own life again. She has created a mission statement for her goals in life and carries it with her to remind herself daily how far she has come.

Judy's story demonstrates one very important principle when it comes to self-confidence and a willingness to recognize your own inner power: The law of control states that you feel good about yourself to the degree you have control over your life. You feel bad about yourself to the extent that other people or events have control over you. You must grip the steering wheel of your life. If you don't assume control of your own life, someone or something else will.

The majority of the people in the world, however, live by the law of accident. They believe there is no control over life, that it's all a matter of luck or who you know. "That's the way the cookie crumbles," they'll sigh. You can spot such people early in a conversation because they never have any goals or plans, they just hope it all works out.

The inner power that is you, however, recognizes that control is achieved by the law of Cause and Effect. This law can be used to keep people from oppressing you. Thoughts are causes. Conditions are effects. If you want to change conditions in the future, you need to change your thoughts in the present. To take control of your life,

> *Act
> as if
> it were impossible
> to fail.*
> —Dorothea Brande

take control of the thoughts in your conscious mind. We choose our emotions and attitudes just as we choose which shoes to wear in the morning.

Inject emotion into your thoughts and they will become your reality faster. Women in my self-defense classes shout *I will fight back* so emotionally and enthusiastically that it rattles the walls.

Affirmations such as *I will fight back* and *I am worth fighting for* reprogram your thinking. Said with enough emotion, these statements are driven deep into your unconscious and overcome previous programming. Whenever you say *I,* be very careful what you say afterwards. Defeating statements such as *I'm tired, I'm afraid* sap your inner strength.

If you believe you are worth fighting for, you will fight. If you believe it, it becomes your reality.

Power, as we've discussed throughout this book, does not mean overpowering other people or asserting control over them. It means what has been called the *power of presence*, which means knowing who you are and being willing to stand up for yourself.

You can exhibit this inner power, as well as back off those who threaten your well-being, by developing the following practices and attitudes with men:

Say no when you mean no

Say yes if you mean yes. A lot of men believe that if they keep pressing, your "no" will become a "yes." Say *no* and put some teeth in it. *No* doesn't have to be explained or apologized for, it's totally self-explanatory. Teasing and hedging can be dangerous and lead to sexual aggression. Be decisive about yes or no and be willing to back up your decision.

You have a right to change your mind

If you are on a date, for example, and you detect danger signals from your companion or the situation, realize that a yes should become a no. Trust your instincts. When you feel threatened or things start to get ugly, change your mind immediately. Leave.

Realize your own self-image

Beware of beliefs, promoted by society or your parents, that hold you back. Beliefs such as: *It's not feminine to get angry....You're not very athletic.....Don't become a tomboy.*

Don't live your life trying to fulfill some other person's ideal of what you're supposed to do, think like, even look like.

Assert Control

Be aware of situations in which you are no longer in control. Change that situation immediately.

"Within every woman there is a wild and natural creature, a powerful force filled with good instincts," wrote Clarissa Pinkola Estes in *Women Who Run With the Wolves.*

She compares women to wolves in being relational by nature, with a great capacity for devotion and being "fiercely stalwart and very brave."

Women's natural power to flourish and be excellent in her own individual manner is her incontestable birthright, says Estes. "Women need not bargain or plead for this. It exists because she exists."

123

12
Men and Power

The measure of man is what he does with power.
—Pittacus

What does it mean for a man to have power in today's society? Is it the financial power that comes with a successful career, an expensive home, "trophy" wife, and all the toys that money can buy? Is it the physical power of athletes or the brutal power of rapists and the violence-prone?

Men often, in fact, find themselves without outer power. A businessman who is a clog in the corporate wheel, or a garbage man, or a teacher, or an artist, may feel financially, physically and mentally powerless.

Some men, frustrated by their lack of power, attempt to obtain it vicariously through the domination or subjugation of others. Examples of immature masculine power in society are the wife beater, the hostile and overbearing boss, the gang member, the coach that ridicules his athletes. Although they perceive their actions as a show of strength, in reality they are demonstrating their own inner anxieties and fear.

Aggressive power has traditionally been associated with men.

There's nothing wrong with aggression in itself, it's whether you use this energy in a positive or negative manner.

Positive expressions of aggression:

- *Decisiveness, knowing that every act and every thought counts.*

- *Commitment to skill and accuracy in work*

- *Standing up for who you are and what you believe*

- *An unconquerable spirit that confronts fear with courage*

Negative expressions of aggression:

- *Physical & mental cruelty*

- *Critical, demanding behaviors*

- *A need to conquer and control others*

- *Addictions & compulsions resulting from anxieties and secret self-loathing*

The martial arts and ancient societies regarded a powerfully aggressive man, a warrior, as possessing far more than physical strength. Inner power, the attributes of courage, discipline, compassion, integrity and self-knowledge were considered essential. In Taekwon-Do, the character traits of courtesy, integrity, perseverance, self-control and indomitable spirit are essential to training.

Three main powers were regarded as "big medicine" by indigenous societies , according to the writer Angeles Arrien:

126

Power of Presence

Every human being has the quality of presence, but for some it is so great that they are called charismatic or magnetic. This power derives from self-knowledge and self-acceptance, as well as the ability to be fully rooted in the present moment—to do what needs to be done now. Woody Allen noted that eighty percent of success is just showing up. The power of presence requires the ability to simply "show up" for what needs to be done.

Power of Communication

Words can heal or destroy. Recently a former client's daughter came to see me. Her mother had rehabilitated her hip at my studio and then returned to the resort that she manages in another country. Now she was back in Phoenix to have a mastectomy because of breast cancer. Her daughter told me through tears that her mother was extremely depressed and wouldn't call me because she thought I would be disappointed in her because she felt weak, indecisive and fearful. "Please call her," the daughter asked, "I know what you say can help her."

It was at that moment that I realized the true power of words. Her daughter saw me as a powerful man, not because of my height or physical strength, but because of compassion and my willingness to say whatever needed to be said to bring her mother out of depression.

To understand and be understood, to say what needs to be said when it needs to be said, grants you effectiveness in every area of your life. Chapter 7 on *Quantum Learning* discusses many ways in which to increase your power of communication.

Power of Position

This does not necessarily mean prestige, but the ability to take a stand, to let others know "this is who I am and what I stand for." All great leaders exhibit this power.

A very old story reveals the depths of power that may be present in an unpretentious and gentle man.

Many years ago there was a tea-server, a very small and polite man, who served tea to all the successful members of Japanese society. He performed his job with care and devotion to detail, honoring all the ancient customs of the art of tea. He used all the proper utensils, which were placed in a precise and prescribed manner.

He went to the market daily to buy the freshest and most exotic teas, which had to be brewed to exactly the right temperature before serving. One day as he rushed about the marketplace buying his teas, he rounded a corner and bumped into the formidable physique of a samurai warrior. The samurai was livid that a lowly tea server had made physical contact with him. The tea-server begged forgiveness. "I was in a hurry and distracted. Please accept my apologies for offending you."

The weak can never forgive. Forgiveness is the attribute of the strong.
—Gandhi

The samurai puffed himself to his full height and responded sternly, "You have brought disrespect to me. There is only one acceptable solution. You must meet me with a sword this afternoon on the field of battle."

"That is certain death for me," said the tea-server. "Please accept my apologies instead. I meant no harm."

The samurai would only be content with the death of the tea-server, and again demanded that he defend himself on the field of battle that afternoon. The tea-server decided to visit a master swordsman. He rapidly assured the master that he did not wish to learn the art of swordsmanship. "I simply want to learn how to die with honor so that I will not bring disrespect to my family."

The master asked him to serve tea first while he pondered the problem. The tea-server prepared tea for the master according to the proper ceremony. The tea-server devoted his attention so thoroughly to the task at hand that he appeared oblivious to the fact that he would be dying in a matter of hours. As the master watched the precise and perfect gestures, he came up with a plan.

"Fetch the sword from my closet," said the master. The tea-server removed the gleaming, heavy blade. The master instructed the tea-server on exactly how he should grip the hilt of the sword with both hands. "When you face the samurai, grip the sword exactly as I have showed you, put the sun over your right shoulder, walk up to the samurai with no conversation, then raise the sword over your head and deliver one strike. The samurai will parry your blow and kill you. But in your attempt, you will bring great respect to your family and you will die with honor."

The tea-server was very happy with these instructions and left with the sword. That afternoon the samurai waited on the field of battle. The tea-server gripped the sword as he had been instructed, found the sun and positioned it over his right shoulder, took a deep breath, strode on to the field and raised the sword high over his head.

The samurai was caught completely off guard. As the blade flashed up and hit the sun, the samurai gasped as he saw the reflection of his own death. He fell to his knees before the tea-server and begged for his life. The tea-server, who had never wished this outcome, instantly decided to spare the samurai.

The master swordsman smiled as he watched secretly from the bushes. He had already realized that the tea-server possessed the spirit of a warrior because he was unafraid to die, wishing only to die with honor. He had also observed the tea-server's focus and attention to

> *Whosoever knows how to fight well is not angry. Whosoever knows how to conquer enemies does not fight them.*
>
> —Tao Te Ching

detail, and knew that he would follow his instructions with no distraction or misdirection. The samurai warrior, who thought he was only going to kill a lowly tea-server, would not be prepared to do battle with such a man.

After that day, the samurai asked to become a student of the tea-server to learn lack of fear and honorable attitudes, and in return he taught the tea-server the art of swordsmanship.

My years in the disciplined, committed, passionate world of Taekwon-Do has taught me this: The greatest victory you can achieve—the only victory you can achieve—is mastery of yourself. It's the purpose of Taekwon-Do. In fact, the word *Master* in the martial arts has a unique meaning, demonstrated by these three lines:

heaven
mortals
earth

Master

The Master is a single line connecting the other three. In other words, the mortal who has united himself with heaven and earth is a Master. He or she has achieved mastery of self by developing spiritual, physical and emotional characteristics that work in harmony within their being. Crushing your opponent or beating him senseless is not the purpose of the martial arts. Rather, it is to control conflict, defend yourself when necessary, and to learn from your opponent's strengths and your own weaknesses. My instructor always told me that self-defense is a by-product of learning the martial arts.

The martial art's discipline, technique and mental training are the mortar for building a strong sense of self, and the ability to proceed with integrity and resolve in the face of all of life's difficulties. Mental

130

conditioning separates the true practitioner from the sensationalist who masters only the fighting aspects of the art. The frenzied explosion of butt-kicking violence that erupts in the movies when some action star battles the enemy is far from the reality of martial arts training. It's merely entertainment.

In fact, Bruce Lee and Chuck Norris, two widely respected martial artists, have embodied martial art in the spiritual and mental sense. Their writing and speech has demonstrated their mental conditioning and discipline.

> *Man who man would be, Must rule the empire of himself.*
>
> —Percy Bysshe Shelley

A common greeting among Taekwon-Do students and teachers is *Pil Sung.* The phrase translates as *I am confident of certain victory.* It does not mean a violent victory over others, but rather the victory over self and all the ways in which we defeat ourselves. It is the embodiment of the tenets of Taekwon-Do: Courtesy, Integrity, Perseverance, Indomitable Spirit and Self-control. *Pil Sung* is a statement of commitment to personal excellence.

Some parents worry that Taekwon-Do may teach violence to boys. In fact, it's just the opposite: they become more social creatures. It teaches them to control their own reactions and, if possible, to defuse violence before it erupts. A truly confident young man has the ability to walk away from a fight without diminishing his self-respect. In competition and the practice studio, the martial arts student can battle an opponent, face fear, experience defeat, learn from mistakes, and then regain balance, learn, grow, and emerge victorious. Overcoming anger, developing mental focus and concentration are all mental tools that are necessary for victory.

With the self-confidence that comes from physical and mental mastery, the urge to fight is lessened, not increased. Studies at Fordham University show that study of the martial arts can curb violent tendencies. It's not about violence, it's about personal self-control.

When I take young men into Taekwon-Do and give them a sense of being able to control their thinking and their physical power, what you see is a heightened sense of social awareness and social behavior. A man without that sense of control and inner power will express himself aggressively and violently in society.

Man's main task in life is to give birth to himself, to become what he potentially is.

—Erich Fromm

Although the martial arts has provided valuable training for myself and many students, it is certainly not the only path to personal power. For a man to acquire the mature inner power that is the birthright of both sexes, he must realize and act upon this one fact: Power, for a man, means having *control over his own life and destiny*.

The purpose of all of your drives for power, for success, for relationships is to feel that you have value, that you are a worthy being. If you look at yourself in the mirror and feel good about what you see, knowing you have met your internal demons and vanquished them, you will feel strong and free.

If a man looks in a mirror and sees a reflection of someone who's not very good at what he does, he feels inadequate, fragile, vulnerable, at risk. A man experiencing that vacuum within himself finds that the negative emotions quickly flow in to fill the empty space. He will often compensate for his own feelings of inadequacy and frustration through violence or aggression. With a diminished sense of control in his own life, he seeks to assert control over others, usually those weaker than him. The less control you have, the fewer freedoms or options you have.

There is only one way to assert control over your own actions and life, and that is to take full responsibility for your success, your happiness and well-being. Healthy self-esteem is not possible without self-responsibility. Men often see responsibility as a burden. I certainly did. It seemed as though full-time responsibility simply required too much effort. It didn't even seem possible. How could I possibly be responsible all the time?

> *The price*
> *of*
> *greatness*
> *is*
> *responsibility.*
> —Winston Churchhill

Gradually I came to understand that the exact opposite is true. Not only is responsibility not a burden, *self-responsibility* to oneself, for oneself, will grant you more freedom, power, security and comfort than you could ever imagine. You can't get any further than you are right now in your business, your relationships, your life, without assuming personal responsibility.

When you exercise self-responsibility, you will like what you see in the mirror every morning. You will look at your reflection and say "*If it's to be, it's up to me.* I can do this. I'm the person responsible. If there's something wrong, I am not going to search for someone to blame, I'm going to ask what am *I* going to do about it?" This is empowering. It puts you in control of your own life. It also gives you a plan.

The speaker John Miller refers to this as "the question behind the question." If the question is "Why didn't I get the result I seek?" then the question behind that is "What can *I* do to get the result?"

The question behind the question always begins with *I*. It never starts with *them* or *they* or *it*.

An irresponsible person is always thinking, "*It's* not my fault. When circumstances change I will be successful," or "when *they* take action, I will be happier." They're always looking for someone or something to blame.

Because I came into the world under difficult circumstances, I used to believe that the world owed me something. Everyone has obstacles and adversity, but for some reason I believed mine were worse. Since destiny or the Creator didn't serve me success and happiness on a platter, I lived irresponsibly. Consequently, I gave up control of my life. My life was like a bumper car at a carnival, careening in different directions depending on whatever bumped against it. Sometimes I could travel in the direction I wanted for a little while, but soon I was swerving in another direction, out of control. It's a very unpredictable and stressful way to live.

Nine years ago I sat with my head in my hands in a one-bedroom apartment, steeped in debt and staring at a bleak future. Suddenly I realized that I had been waiting for someone to come and save me. Someone to arrive out of the blue and tell me what to do, or give me money, or just show me a direction. That's when I realized the secret that would turn my life around: *No one was going to come and save me.* No one is going to come and save you. You can sit around and wait for something to happen if you want to, or you can get up, create an action plan, and get busy with your life. It is 100% up to you to save yourself. You are responsible for becoming the person you were born to be.

Learn to say three very powerful words: *I am responsible.* The weather is not responsible, my boss is not responsible, my spouse is not responsible, *I am responsible.* To be able to say with total conviction *I am responsible* removes stress instantly and clarifies your thinking.

Throughout my life, I've come in contact with many role models, who by their actions and words have shown me key elements in developing self-responsibility. Although there are many completions to the sentence *I am responsible*, here are the seven key phrases they have taught me to place behind the words *I am responsible.* If you will say these seven affirmations to yourself every morning, and put them into practice in your daily routine, not only will your life change, *it will change immediately.*

1. I am responsible for the person I am today and the person I am becoming.

I am responsible for the achievement of my goals and desires. No one owes me the fulfillment of my wishes. No one owes me happiness. I do not hold a mortgage on anyone else's life and they hold no obligation towards mine. If I have dreams and goals, it's up to me to discover how to satisfy them. I must take responsibility for developing and implementing an action plan.

No one is going to come and save me. If my goals require participation from other people, I need to find out who those people are and what they need from me in order to reach my goal. I must provide what they need. I will find a way to compensate them for their help. I must ask for help, not wait for it to be delivered. If it's to be, it's up to me.

2. I am responsible for my choices and my actions.

I am responsible for my choices, not in the sense of moral guilt or blame, but as the chief cause of my own destiny.

If a friend commits suicide, I do not feel guilty and keep thinking *if only I could have done this or said that...* Guilt implies choice and responsibility. In areas where we have no choice, we can have no guilt. We can have regret, but not guilt. We are only responsible where we have a choice. I do not blame myself by looking backwards at what has already happened and cannot be changed in any event. I look forward because I know that I am creating my own future by my decisions and actions now. I am responsible. If I take full responsibility for my choices and actions today, I won't have to make excuses for myself tomorrow. I will do what I am supposed to do, when I am supposed to do it. I will say what I'm supposed to say when I'm supposed to say it.

I won't have to apologize so often. I won't be tempted to cast blame on other people or circumstances. When I take full responsibility for my choices and actions, I experience peace of mind.

3. I am responsible for my attitude.

To truly achieve power, you must feel in complete control over your attitude at all times. There is a saying among psychologists that you must take responsibility for what you're not responsible for. In other words, although you are not responsible for the parents, teachers or others who wounded you as a child, or you're not responsible for the driver who runs a red light and sideswipes your car, you are responsible for the attitude you choose in dealing with these problems.

4. I am responsible for the attitude that I bring to my work.

I will give my work the best I have to give, for I see my work as an expression of who I am. I see my work as representing me.

In the past, workers were often referred to as craftsmen. Their work was signed, identified. People wanted to buy certain pieces of furniture or clothing created by craftsman who were known for their conscientious attitude in producing an excellent product. Sometimes we see the exact opposite of that today: men trying to get by on as little work as possible. True responsibility says that I will consider the ways in which my work can affect other people's lives and I will bring that level of awareness and focus to my work.

I know what I'm supposed to do. I'm responsible to do it.

5. I am responsible for the attitude that I bring to my relationships.

As we discuss in Chapter 14, you will probably find that relationships will create 85% of your happiness in life. Too often men expect other people to make us happy. We place the total responsibility for the relationship on our girlfriend or spouse, on our employees or coworkers, on our friends. I am especially responsible for the attitude I bring to my relationship with my children and my spouse. If I realize there is a difficulty in my relationship, I will be a responsible person and initiate discussion. I will not wait for my wife or girlfriend to deal with it. All my relationships require my active participation and I am responsible for the behavior, thoughts and emotions that I bring to my relationships..

6. I am responsible for the quality of my communication.

I must accept responsibility for the things that I say. I am responsible for the attitude that I bring to my conversations. I will not withdraw or "stonewall" my life partner or business associates when discussion needs to take place.

Men often deny the power of their words. Sometimes we even deny that we remember saying something particularly hurtful. Damaging words live on. They may be forgiven, but they are rarely forgotten. When I say something that is particularly harmful or hurtful, I must recognize this and make amends, say "I'm sorry." Sometimes the damage can't be undone, but I still need to convey my understanding of how my words have hurt another person.

I am responsible for fully understanding what the other person is saying by listening attentively, patiently, without interruption. I will listen on a deeper level to their words by paraphrasing what I think I am hearing, or asking open-ended questions when necessary. When I am the one speaking, I am responsible for making sure I am understood by speaking clearly and decisively, and by using examples.

7. I am responsible for my happiness.

I do not expect a wife, girlfriend or lover to make me happy. No one else is responsible for my happiness but me. I must do the things that I know will result in building my sense of self-worth and my values, and I must continue to do them on an ongoing basis. My self-esteem and happiness at this point in my life are the direct result of the values I have chosen to accept. If I am unhappy, I need to choose a different set of values by which to live.

I realize it's very difficult to assume full responsibility for your own life. It's always easier to blame someone else and hope someone else will do for you what you are unwilling to do for yourself. The rewards, however, are beyond belief. As George Bernard Shaw said, you will become "a force of nature instead of a feverish selfish little clod of ailments and grievances complaining that the world will not devote itself to making you happy."

Self-responsibility will empower you beyond your expectations. You will be able to face your reflection in the mirror without fear or doubt, with the quiet assurance and positive attitude of someone who can say: *I know who I am and what I am capable of accomplishing. I am responsible. I am in control of my life.* You will be able to say, in the words of William Henley:

> *I am the master of my fate:*
> *I am the captain of my soul.*

13
Loving Yourself

If there is no enemy within,
the enemy without can do us no harm.
—African proverb

Without love and respect for yourself, you cannot respect others. The golden rule in the Bible—as well as all the other major religious texts of the world—states that we should love others *as* ourselves. Not better than, not less than, but *as* we love ourselves. The need to love yourself seems implicit to me in this commandment, for how can I respect or love you if I don't even like myself?

You also need to love yourself in order to be able to accept and appreciate the love that flows from others. People used to say I was very difficult to love. When I was in my early twenties, if a girlfriend tried to hold my hand while walking down the street, I could only tolerate it for a minute or so before I would wiggle loose. Her hand almost burned. Since I saw myself as unworthy, I viewed the love others gave me with skepticism.

As Groucho Marx said, "I wouldn't belong to any club that would have me as a member."

As long as you continue to dislike yourself, you will continue with negative habits, like overeating, drinking, slovenly work practices. When you develop a solid self-love, those behaviors will seem foreign to you because you simply like yourself too much to subject yourself to such things.

When we choose to treat ourselves with respect, it is the voice of the life-force within us. It is selfishness in the most noble meaning of the word selfish. If that voice goes silent, the first thing that will die is self-esteem.

Self-acceptance is a refusal to be in an adversarial relationship with yourself. Self-esteem is impossible without self-acceptance. If you are capable of self-acceptance, you will fight for your life even when filled with despair. Self-acceptance will lead you in the depths of depression to go to a therapist. After years of suffering abuse, self-acceptance can finally lead you to shout "No! I'm not going to take this any more"

> *It is the highest form of self-respect to admit mistakes and to make amends for them.*
> —John J. McCloy

Sometimes we deny our own emotions or behavior. Maybe you have thoughts that creep into your mind. They're unwanted but you can't get rid of them. Why? Because you haven't accepted them as part of you. No progress is possible until you have first accepted your own reality, "warts and all," as Shakespeare says. You must be able to stand in the middle of yourself and say "This is who I am."

To accept negative emotions is more than simply to acknowledge or admit them. Open yourself to them, stand in their midst and *experience* their reality. Own them, say *they're mine*. Even if you are ashamed of certain actions, you must still pause in the presence of what you know to be true.

Accepting does not mean enjoying or condoning. Accepting does not mean that your emotions will have the last word. I may get up in the morning and not feel like going to work. I don't rationalize my feelings or call myself lazy, I simply acknowledge that feeling, feel that feeling, then get up and go to work.

Denied feelings fight for mental space and recognition, preventing concentration and focus. When you fully experience your negative feelings, you've allowed them to have their say—their moment on the stage— and then often they will leave easily. You can begin your day without struggling with self-deception.

Before you can achieve self-esteem, before you can start liking yourself, first you must work on acceptance. Self-acceptance is a fundamental precondition for growth or change. The three levels of self-acceptance are:

1.   I am *"for"* myself in the most fundamental sense, simply because I am alive. This level is a more primitive or primal form of self-esteem. It is the natural birthright of every human being, and yet we have the ability to nullify or negate it.

2.   *Willingness to experience* without denial or evasion that what we think, we think. We feel what we feel, we desire what we desire. We have done what we have done. It is the refusal to regard any part of ourselves, our thoughts, our behaviors, our dreams as "not me." I may not like everything I see or want to repeat certain behaviors, but they were mine at that point in time.

141

3. Compassion. At this level I can become a friend to myself. If I do something that I regret, of which I feel ashamed, I want to understand why something that was wrong or inappropriate felt desirable or appropriate at that time. What internal thoughts or considerations went into creating that behavior? There's always a context under which the most offensive actions can make their own kind of sense.

At this third level, we want to know *why,* not to justify or judge, but to understand, forgive and move on. I can condemn an action I've taken and still have compassion for the motives that prompted it. This has nothing to do with providing alibis, rationalizing, or avoiding responsibility for our actions.

> *The shortest and surest way to live with honor in the world is to be in reality what we would appear to be.*
>
> —Socrates

Integrity is one of the tenets of Taekwon-Do. Integrity is essential to self-esteem. A dictionary definition of integrity is "the quality or condition of being whole or undivided; completeness." In other words, your actions must match your words. When behavior is congruent with your expressed values, you have integrity. You have one face, no matter who you're talking to, no matter where you are.

"Loss of face" is a failure to live up to one's own standards. In the Orient, loss of face may be so severe that one commits suicide. We commit a slower suicide in the West when we don't practice integrity. Lack of integrity wounds our self-esteem. We lose respect for ourselves and start to call ourselves names or negatively criticize ourselves. *I am so stupid. Can't I get anything right?* The mind has betrayed itself, and so we gradually treat ourselves worse and worse until we have become the thing we despise most: a failure, a "loser."

Integrity means congruence. Studies show that in the workplace, many people do not trust their bosses. Why do you trust certain people and not others? The answer is congruency—their actions match their words.

When I was twelve years old, I quickly spotted incongruence in the adults at the church I attended. On Sunday, they would talk about honesty, compassion and love. Yet the moment they stepped out of that church, they resumed lying, cheating on their spouses, and dishonest business practices. Another word for incongruence is hypocrisy. Children spot hypocrisy instantly. Certain adults can be trusted, while others cannot. Children may not be able to articulate what they know, but they *know*.

In a speech to a group of executives, I gave them this sentence stem: If I want people to perceive me as trustworthy I........... "Give me six responses to that question," I asked them. What are the six you would list? They are an indication of the values you hold, and the behaviors you must perform in order to achieve integrity. The most consistent answers among the executives were:

> I must keep my word.
> I must walk my talk.
> I must follow through on my commitments.
> I must be consistent.
> I must protect my employees.

If I pretend to listen to my employees' ideas when my mind is already made up, if I ask for honest feedback then penalize the employee who gives it to me, if I preach quality, but provide shoddy services or products, if I respond with righteous indignation when others don't follow through on their promises, yet don't keep

*Be not
simply good;
be good
for something.*

— Thoreau

my own, I have attacked *myself* in a way that no verbal attack or rejection from society can. Hypocrisy is self-betrayal. The mind betrays the mind.

Sometimes you may be caught in a clash of values and the right answer may not be readily apparent. Integrity does not guarantee that you will make the best choice or the "right choice." As long as your search for the right answer is sincere, is authentic, you stay connected with the virtue of integrity. You take responsibility for your choices and the consequences of your actions.

One of the worst rationalizations I have used

> *Do not say things.*
> *What you are*
> *stands over you*
> *the while,*
> *and thunders,*
> *so that I cannot hear*
> *what you say*
> *to the contrary.*
>
> —Ralph Waldo Emerson

in the past is that "It's okay to tell a lie because only I know I lied. Only I know that I didn't fulfill my promise." That idea states loud and clear that my opinion is unimportant and only the opinion of others will count.

When it comes to matters of self-esteem, I have more to fear from my own judgment than from anyone else's. At the center of my consciousness is the judge from whom there is no escape. I can avoid people who have learned humiliating truth about me but I cannot avoid myself.

Most of the choices we make when it comes to integrity are not great ones, yet the accumulated weight of these choices has a tremendous impact on the sense of self. The little things add up. We become the daily choices we make.

Employees who take office supplies....parents who won't admit when they're wrong to their children....managers who pad their expense accounts. If you make those choices, you are slowly and surely heading down the road of hypocrisy and self-loathing. Self-esteem will be impossible.

Many of these "little" choices will set you securely on the path to inner power that comes from integrity, self-esteem and a healthy self-love. Truth will become a way of life:

- Don't laugh at jokes that are stupid and vulgar.
- Expend more effort at work.
- Follow through on promises.
- Don't just say what people want to hear.
- Say no when you really want to say no.
- Acknowledge responsibility to people you have hurt. Make amends.
- Remind yourself daily, *If it's to be, it's up to me.*

You can show yourself love in many ways:

Take care of yourself

Tend to the body through diet, exercise and sleep. Tend to the mind by providing periods of "downtime," relaxation and pleasurable activities. Good health is essential to your well-being and success as a whole person.

Recognize your worth

Recognize your own worth simply because you exist. Feelings of being undeserving can sabotage your best efforts. Have you ever worked hard towards an important goal, put in lots of hours, study, research, but just when the goal was in sight, you made some fatal mistake that doomed your efforts to failure?

Or do you ever get success anxiety when things start going well? *If I'm this happy, something's bound to go wrong.* If that attitude continues, you will do something to prevent your success, so that you can get back to being comfortable in your rut.

You deserve happiness and success. Celebrate the uniqueness of your own life. You do not require anyone else's validation. God provided you with your validation when you were born.

Act your way into confidence

As I've said before, when all else fails, act "as if" you are a confident, self-accepting person. Ask yourself, *If I actually felt confident in myself, how would I behave in this situation? How would (a confident role model that I know) behave?* Then do it.

Practice affirmative action

Many people use affirmations, either written or spoken, to etch a statement in the unconscious mind. You can use whatever affirmations have the most meaning to you, but they must be three things:

Personal: *I* am strong and confident.

Present tense: I *am* confident of certain victory

Positive: Use words like *I am, I can, I will.* Avoid guilt-inducing phrases like *have to* or *should.* Never employ negative words such as *can't* or *stop* or *don't.*

Affirmations are simply telling the truth in advance:

I am the regional sales manager.

I am patient.

I can do it.

I feel terrific.

Say affirmations enthusiastically. Say them out loud and in the mirror, whenever possible. Changes are immediate. This doesn't take a month or three months. Your behavior, tone of voice, gestures will change. Often other people will notice changes in you before you do.

Affirmations access your subconscious directly. Sometimes people are uncomfortable with mental programming. Yet you do it already, all day long. As Emerson said, you become what you think about all day long. If you are thinking *I'm tired, I'm afraid*, your subconscious mind will spin these thoughts into your reality.

Why not feed your mind instead with the things you want, the ideas you're creating, the goals you've set for yourself? Your mind will accept as true whatever you tell it.

Play the "I Like Me" Game

I have spoken to groups of abused or neglected children and asked them to play the "I like me" game. It begins with a statement "I like me" said silently, whispered softly, then shouted into the room. As that statement is affirmed over and over, body language changes. They look outward instead of at the floor, their faces break out in smiles, their postures become alert.

Many of these children have never experienced the validation of having someone else like them or love them, so now they are brimming with enthusiasm at the idea of liking themselves.

Try standing in front of a mirror and saying out loud "I like myself." Over and over. You may feel foolish at first, but the words will soon begin to take root in your unconscious mind.

One man questioned me during a speech about the "I like me" affirmation. "I know people who like themselves so well that all they can talk about are their ideas and their accomplishments," he said. "Is there a danger that liking yourself too much can lead to arrogance?"

Liking yourself does not mean that you must convince others of your likability. Arrogant people who spend a great deal of time talking about themselves in reality do not like themselves very much at all. They are most likely very insecure and searching for your approval to fill the cracks in their own self-esteem.

Liking yourself breeds confidence and realistic self-acceptance. Arrogance leads to stagnation of growth because of a belief in your own perfection.

Forgive yourself

You are a human being, and no matter how hard you try, you're going to occasionally screw up. You are capable of excellence, but you are not capable of perfection. When you like yourself and accept yourself fully, you are able to forgive yourself for the mistakes and failures along the way.

Life changes so rapidly that you are probably facing at least one new crisis or challenge right now. The self-love that will carry you through these times has been compared to the parent's love for a child. The psychologist Carl Rogers calls it "*unconditional* positive regard." This means that you value and respect yourself regardless of your origins, past failures or achievements, talents, shape or size.

It's also been said that we tend to treat others the way we feel about ourselves. If you value and respect yourself, behaving with integrity, you will treat others better as well. If you do not like yourself, you will not be open to the love and support that will flow to you from others. A solid foundation of self-respect opens the door to healthy, loving relationships, as we will see in the following chapters.

14

Loving the Other

If we discovered that we had only five minutes left to say
all we wanted to say,
every telephone booth would be occupied
by people calling each other
to stammer that they loved them.
—Christopher Morley

Your ability to give and receive love is the greatest of life's gifts. You will get 85% of all your joy in life, I believe, from your interactions with other people, and only 15% from your earned success.

A satisfying intimacy with a spouse or significant other can be a major source of happiness and comfort. A fulfilling, soul-satisfying relationship with one other human being is probably the most desired goal in our society, and yet the most difficult to achieve.

Marriages and successful relationships do not occur easily or automatically just because you are in love. We live in a hectic, time-driven culture in which the needs of a relationship frequently take back seat to the demands of bosses, work, children, and other family

> *Love doesn't grow on the trees like apples in Eden— it's something you have to make.*
>
> —Joyce Cary

members. However, psychologists and researchers who study the reasons for high divorce rates and failed relationships have discovered there are several predictors for a happy and stable relationship.

Five key elements can ignite faltering and troubled relationships. At the heart of these behavioral changes is the realization that love is a verb. It's an action word, not a passive state. You do not accidentally *fall* in love, you *create* love by your own actions.

Commit yourself 100%.

Women as well as men can be "commitment-phobes." Committing yourself to another person is scary. Maybe the other person will turn out to be unworthy of the commitment. Or maybe he or she will reject you. The happiest outcome would be that you will find a stability, power and strength together that will carry you through the most turbulent waters of life.

Take the quantum leap into total commitment. The risk of rejection or loss is always present. You may get hurt, you may be rejected, but stack that up against the odds of what will happen if you don't take that risk: A lonely life, a mediocre life, a bland life.

Lack of commitment is evidenced by statements such as "Let's try" rather than "We will make it work." In weddings I've recently attended, I don't as often hear the pledge "until death do us part." Now I hear phrases such as "I promise to be with you as long as we both shall love each other." Isn't that much more realistic, you may ask? No, because there are times within the relationship that you may not love or even like that other person, you may in fact hate them. Without a loving commitment to stay through the bad times, you'll either split or go find another partner. You can easily be led astray by another attraction if you are not committed to the relationship, and you'll end up creating the same mess you're in now because you didn't address the basic problems of relationship.

You cannot get a relationship to work unless you are willing to do whatever it takes, including forsaking all others.

A lack of commitment often leads to power struggles. The need to be "right" or in control leads to resentment and jockeying for the dominant position. In an effort to balance the power, couples often develop an "I'll go-halfway" mentality. Sometimes people that live together arrange to split all expenses exactly fifty-fifty. I knew a couple who went so far as to tag furniture and other household items, "which is mine, which is yours." They were already prepared for the breakup in advance. All they had to do was walk through and pick out their things.

The flaw in the halfway mentality is that, at times, one person may slack off. Perhaps one person is overwhelmed at work and soon is giving only 40%. Because that's not "fair," the other party digs in and also starts giving less. A rift grows into a canyon of neglect until they quit trying altogether.

Lack of commitment is also demonstrated by a marriage contract or prenuptial agreement. This is a controversial subject with athletes I've talked to because they feel they need to protect what they've acquired. Yet a prenuptial agreement plans the details of the separation even before you get married. It tells one partner that they may not be completely trusted or worthy of the person they are marrying. An attorney I know has written a great many prenuptial agreements. He states that over the last ten years, over 92% of all the marriages involving prenuptial agreements have failed in the first three years.

Jump in with both feet. Never consider the possibility of the relationship failing. If through no fault of your own the relationship does not work out, at least you will know you were not halfhearted about it.

Improve yourself, not the other person

Most couples in troubled relationships believe that substantial changes need to be made, and usually by the other person. "If he or she would just lose weight, be more communicative, quit smoking, think more positively.... it would all work out," they believe.

Love is an act of endless forgiveness.
—Peter Ustinov

Trying to change the other person is a subtle form of personal rejection, a way of saying, "you're not quite good enough the way you are." When you try to force people to change, they will dig in their heels, become hostile, defensive, and resist change with all their energy. The fact is that people do not change very much. Like Flip Wilson used to say "What you see is what you get."

The first ingredient for change has to be desire on the part of the person changing. When you stop trying to change the other person and just accept them unconditionally as they are, you lay the groundwork for the possibility that they may transform of their own choice.

Work on yourself, improve your own relationship skills, and you will create a change in yourself that your partner will now have to react to differently. Even small changes in your behavior can make a big difference in the way your partner perceives you and reacts to you.

Face your fears

Nearly everyone has ended a relationship at one time or another because they suspected the other person was ready to leave, and they wanted to be first. We fear rejection, we fear being laughed at, humiliation, failure, and every other threat to our self-esteem. Fear leads to jealousy, possessiveness, controlling behavior, all the attributes that sink a relationship.

Jealousy, for example, usually arises from your own insecurities rather than the other person's behavior. If you feel inadequate or unworthy, if you were frequently put down or criticized as a child, if you suffered from lack of love or the threat of love's withdrawal, you are particularly prey to the "green-eyed monster." Your partner might be very much in love with you, but because of your own feelings of unworthiness you will simply not be able to accept that love, and assume they must be searching for someone "better."

Deal with your own self-esteem rather than asserting jealousy and other controlling behaviors into the relationship. When you like and accept yourself sincerely, then nothing that anyone else does or does not do will ever make you doubt yourself or your own personal value. You will be emotionally self-reliant.

Create positive expectations for your partner

This rule is simple: Expect the best of your partner. Perhaps the most wonderful phrase that a person can say to their partner is "I love you. I believe in you. I know you can do it."

Your expectations have a tendency to be fulfilled, whether positive or negative. If you expect your partner to let you down, seldom will you be disappointed.

One psychologist, Howard Markman at the University of Denver, has found in his research that the number of negative behaviors in a relationship can predict divorce. So powerful is a destructive thought that one "zinger" or put-down erases 20 positive acts of kindness, he asserts.

Other researchers have noted that the four primary relationship killers are criticism, contempt, defensiveness and withdrawal.

Criticism and contempt create a downward spiral until the other person either gets defensive or completely withdraws. It is the surest way to poison love.

Remember your partner's good qualities, even in the heat of battle. Always remind him or her that you have complete faith in their ability to do anything that they put their minds to. Always expect the best. You will be amazed at the results.

Keep lines of communication open

First of all, *listen.* One of our greatest needs is to be listened to and understood. Several recent bestselling books have focused on the problems of communication between men and women. Your partner perceives the world in a very different way than you do. Without listening skills, you will not hear the feelings and thoughts behind the words.

Particularly when a relationship becomes stormy, we often quit listening to the other person because we are so sure we're "right." When you finally negotiate the peace you find out that usually there's a misunderstanding at the base of it. Do everything you can to make sure lines of communication remain open. Don't be afraid to ask silly questions. Pin your partner down and ask them, "What did you mean by that?" Challenge their body language or tone of voice if it seems to provide a different meaning. "I hear you saying that you want to go out to dinner tonight, but your voice sounds angry. Is this true?" Perhaps your mate's voice and body language are reflecting a bad day at work rather than annoyance at you, but if you don't ask, and *listen* to the answer, you'll never know. Reread the chapter on enhancing your listening skills, if necessary.

Secondly, don't be afraid to *talk*. Letting someone else into your emotional world is an act of trust. It tells them that they are important enough that you will share your deepest feelings with them. If you become defensive and withdraw because of perceived criticisms, your partner may never understand why you are so unhappy until the day you walk out the door. Give the relationship a chance by communicating your needs to your partner in an open, nonthreatening way.

Are You Incompatible?

Couples often believe they are incompatible because of behavioral differences. "He likes to go out and party, I like to stay home." Or "I'm a morning person and he's a night owl." These incompatibilities are not facts, but problems which are amenable to negotiation and solutions.

Only one true incompatibility exists, and that is when there is truly no desire on the part of one or both people to save the relationship. Usually this happens when there is no love present. Either they were not in love at the beginning, or they married for the wrong reasons, or their love has been so thoroughly annihilated by negative behaviors that home has become an armed camp of misery and entrapment.

In real love you want the other person's good. In romantic love you want the other person.

—Margaret Anderson

Some relationships must end. Not everyone is capable of the commitment, empathy and hard work that may be necessary to save a marriage. The presence of addictions or abuse may also doom the relationship.

William James said that the first step to dealing with any difficulty is to be willing to have it so. Unhappiness, stress, tension, depression and psychosomatic illness arise by living in a state of denial, by refusing to face an unpleasant reality.

155

An unhappy relationship can shred you emotionally, undermine your will to succeed and destroy your potential probably more than any other single factor. Do everything possible to build and maintain a loving relationship. If it doesn't work out, have the courage and character to accept that nothing in human life is either perfect or permanent. Life is what it is and not as you wish it would be.

Here are three really bad reasons for staying in a loveless marriage:

You're afraid of what others will say

The fact is that no one else really cares as much about your relationship as you do. Friends are concerned about your well-being, but a divorce will not shake them up to the degree you think it will. They have their own problems and concerns.

You're staying together "for the sake of the children"

Children are often used as an excuse to delay the inevitable. Yet children will probably be better off as a recipient of love from a single caring parent, rather than as the innocent victims of a loveless atmosphere of guerrilla warfare and constant sniping. Children derive their ideas about how a relationship is supposed to work from watching their parents. Particularly if there is verbal or physical abuse in the home, you must realize the impact this will have on your children's future interactions with others.

You don't want to hurt your partner by leaving.

You can't really make anyone else happy when you're unhappy, because the only thing you've got to give is bitterness and frustration. Only happy people can make other people happy. Don't sacrifice yourself on the altar of someone else's happiness.

However, true incompatibility is rarer than you would think. Most perceived incompatibilities are in reality problems or challenges that are amenable to your intelligence and positive behavior. People change the most dramatically between 21 and 31 years of age. If you were married right out of high school or college, you are probably living with someone vastly different than you married. Perhaps you've thought *He is not the person I married* or *she is turning out just like her mother.*

Probably you've both grown in new directions, developed new tastes and interests. That's neither good nor bad, it just is. Nobody is at fault, because we all inevitably grow and change. Change does not need to be a threat, it can be an adventure. You can discover and fall in love with an entirely new person.

A good marriage requires not only commitment, but the ability to change and welcome change in the other person. In other words, you must move along in this relationship if it is to last.

Rekindling the Fires

Love is not a matter of falling in love and staying in love, rather falling in love and then developing a respect and a liking. The liking lasts during the time when you're not in love. You may fall in and out of love with the same person many times over the course of a long term relationship.

If you were in love at one time, and you're now willing, then your marriage can be saved. The relationship may not be hopeless, it may just be going through a change. It may be ready to move to another level of enjoyment, a higher level of experience. Even in the most devastated battlegrounds of love, there is still an ember or spark ready to be fanned into a fire.

The Greek had a word for the rekindling process: *praxis.*

The principle of praxis states that you generate emotion in yourself by doing things consistent with those emotions over and over until they rekindle into flame. You act your way into the feeling until it becomes your reality.

> *Ecstasy cannot last, but it can carve a channel for something lasting.*
> —E.M. Forster

Relationships can be more enjoyable after they've been rekindled than they were in the beginning. Those who have been married 15, 20, even 50 years or more say their marriage enters a new honeymoon and becomes an intense emotional love affair. Love, no longer taken for granted, now glows deeper and richer. They are truly appreciative of the person who has stuck with them for all these years. They love each other as they are now, not as they used to be.

It is very easy to fall back in love with a person that you were once in love with. To rekindle love through your everyday behaviors, you must first act as a person in love would act. Don't just sit back and wait to "feel" in love, rather act your way into the feeling. You begin to love another person by doing loving things with and for that person. Small things, small attentions, little favors, little kindnesses, make that other person feel happy and rekindle your own love in the process.

Remembering that the word love is a verb, begin adding the little acts of thoughtful kindness that tell the other person you love them: compliment your partner on how he or she looks, hug your mate, surprise them with a small gift or flowers, listen to your partner attentively. Do the things you did during courtship. Be more sympathetic, more attentive, more understanding. As you act the role of a lover, your feelings for the other person will begin to change for the better. You are now in the process of acting your way back into love and it happens very fast.

Subtract from your relationship the acts of thoughtless nastiness, such as withdrawing when you are angry, or calling your partner names.

Students in physical training know that, once they get into shape, they are going to have to maintain it by continuing to do the things they did in the first place to get there. Likewise, love is not a static state. If you're going to stay in love, you need to do the things you did to fall into love in the first place.

Never take love for granted. I've had friends tell me, " I don't need to say I love her, she knows I love her." But you need to say it. Just as words can hurt, so can they heal.

> *Love is a force....*
> *It is not a result;*
> *it is a cause.*
> *It is not a product.*
> *It is a power,*
> *like money,*
> *or steam*
> *or electricity.*
> *It is valueless*
> *unless you can*
> *give something else*
> *by means of it.*
> —Anne Morrow Lindbergh

Say "I love you" as passionately and as often as possible. Love is the greatest inner power you can manifest. Love requires both defiance and surrender, for it is the ultimate affirmation of life.

15
Lo ving the World

Not one of us knows what effect his life produces,
and what he gives to others;
that is hidden from us and must remain so,
though we are often allowed to see some
little fraction of it, so that we may not lose courage.
The way in which power works is a mystery.
—Albert Schweitzer

This is not an easy world to live in. This is not an easy world in which to be honest, to be committed, to be self-confident, to be caring. Yet live in it you must, because you are part of a functioning whole, a holistic system. You will never accomplish anything totally alone and you will never change without affecting some change in the lives of those around you. Scientists may call it systems theory, spiritualists may call it the world soul, oversoul, or cosmic consciousness, but it amounts to the same thing. We are not islands, we are drops of a single ocean.

Even the smallest actions, the little acts of character have a ripple effect in the world. What you put into the world will also eventually flow back to you in kind. It's sometimes called the law of reciprocity, or the law of karma. As the Bible says, "As ye sow, so shall ye reap."

I find in the universe so many forms of order, organization, system, law; and adjustment of means to ends, that I believe in a cosmic intelligence and I conceive God as the life, mind, order, and law of the world.

—Will Durant

We are spiritual as well as mental and physical beings. Spiritual faith has been the source of power for countless great men and women of history. Faith is an antidote to the fears that prey on us, the self-doubts that sabotage our best efforts. Faith creates; doubt and fear destroy. Faith, said the philosopher William James, creates our reality, the actual facts of our existence.

Whatever your faith, make it an intrinsic part of your life. Let loving and ethical precepts guide your actions toward the world around you. Although your faith can literally move mountains, remember it still requires your effort and choice, not merely wishful thinking.

There's a old Zen story about two monks strolling through the forest one day. Suddenly a snarling Bengal tiger appeared on the path, blocking their way. The older monk remained calm in the face of this disaster. "You must merely have faith," he assured the younger monk. "We are holy men of God and He shall not allow us to be harmed by this tiger."

The younger monk promptly spun on his heels and took off running. When the old monk finally caught up to him, he demanded "Have you no faith? God would have kept us safe from danger. He has complete control of that tiger."

"I know He does," his companion replied. "But why should I bother

God about that tiger when He gave me two legs that can run so fast?"

Growing, striving, accomplishing, taking care of your own needs, doesn't imply a lack of faith. It simply means that you respect the universe enough not to demand what you are unwilling to go to the effort of obtaining yourself.

At the most basic level of our relationship with the world should be simple respect. Respect means:

Respect for our family, partners, associates and friends

True courtesy means that we take them seriously and at face value, not secretly doubting the motives behind everything they say, but listening quietly and communicating in return.

Respect for teachers and mentors

The formal bowing to the martial arts instructor is something that sometimes rankles with modern students. It is more than a quaint old custom, however, it is the mark of respect for a teacher as the embodiment of the values he represents, regardless of age. A 30 year-old white belt will bow with respect to a 12 year-old black belt. Respect your teachers.

Respect for children

Children spell *love* as *t-i-m-e*. If we don't spend time with them, then we must not love them or think they are worthwhile. The time we most need to express our emotions positively with kids is when they are the most exasperating. We need to force ourselves to smile, to say "Come here and give me a hug. You know I love you. Always have and always will. I don't like this behavior and I'm going to do something about that, but there is nothing you can do that will ever make me stop loving you."

163

Respect for strangers

It's a lot easier to show respect for those we love than those we regard as strangers or "not like us." Even strangers can be our teachers, however, and so courtesy demands that we remain open to them. Be outgoing, force yourself to put a smile on your face. Don't retreat inside yourself and hide. When things get tough and it seems that the pressure and stress of ordinary life and expectations and deadlines and budgets and goals are starting to bear down on us and the noise level is going up all around you and there never seems to be enough time in the day, those are the times to open up instead of retreating.

In the faces of men and women I see God.
—Walt Whitman

Respect for Creation

Give something back. Learn to live with a sense of service. Many devote time to environmental causes, to building homes for the homeless and feeding the hungry, to wildlife and animals. Charles Dickens said that no one is useless in this world who lightens the burden for someone else. We are rich through what we give away and poor through what we keep. Reach out to the world with respect, for nothing more in return than a good feeling inside yourself.

In Phoenix I involve myself in a lot of different charities, Aid to Adoption for Special Kids, Cystic Fibrosis, the Arthritis Foundation. I do lectures in high schools and homeless shelters, for kids especially. People ask why I give so much of my time. Because a medic on the battlefield ran out and pulled me in. I have no idea who he was or where he is, but I have a debt that I must pay back. There must be

When you cease to make a contribution you begin to die.
—Eleanor Roosevelt

164

some reason I am still here because there were so many times I could have died. It is my job to uncover all of my potentials, it is my job to fulfill my talents, it is my job to open every gift the good Lord gave me.

As you increase the actions that show respect and love for the world, you will find that you genuinely like and respect yourself and are able to accept the love of others. You will have peace of mind.

As we discussed in the last chapter, 85% of your joy in life will probably arise from your relationships with other people. In developing our human relationships, the goal is to get along with lots of different types of people and personalities. I used to be able to get along only with people who were just like me or people who were more or less willing to play down their own personalities in favor of mine.

The most successful and happy men and women are those who make those around them feel good about themselves. One way to tell whether you value other people and express your regard for them is this: Do their eyes light up when you enter the room? Do they automatically smile and look genuinely glad to see you?

When you take every opportunity possible to improve the health and personality of another person, you will be doing the same for yourself. Everything you do to raise someone else's self-esteem raises your own at the same time and in the same measure.

The law of indirect effort also comes into play. If you want to be happy, the direct method would be to do whatever you think will make you happy. The indirect method is to make others happy. To the extent that you have brightened the lives of others, so will you find your spirits lifted and self-esteem increase. If you are sincerely impressed with someone else, the more likely they are to be impressed by you. The more you respect others, the more they respect you.

Positive behavior towards other people requires the five A's:

Be Agreeable

This simply means eliminating the three C's from your interactions: criticizing, complaining and condemning. Keep a pleasant expression on your face and use positive body language when meeting someone or listening to them.

Being agreeable doesn't mean that you're a "yes" person or that you necessarily agree with what someone else says. It means that you are respectfully allowing the other person to have their say.

I used to argue all the time. Arguing was natural, even healthy, I thought. Extensive reading assured me of the rightness of my opinions. I wanted to let everyone know how right I was. Arguing was a way to build my self-esteem, even if it sometimes resulted in ridiculing others.

Consequently, I spent a lot of time alone. Once in college I watched a group of people seemingly evaporate into thin air rather than have me join their group. Finally I decided to stop trying to be so right all the time. I had won many arguments, but eliminated conversation. I still love spirited conversation, only now I love to hear the opinions of other people as well.

Is it so important for you to always be right? Instead, ask yourself "Does this work? Is this effective?" Others will find you far more agreeable and pleasant.

Acceptance

We all seek the acceptance of other people. Babies and children look into the face of their mothers and fathers to see if they are accepted as important or loved or funny or intelligent. We have a deep need to be accepted by other people, even people we don't know. The easiest and best way to show someone you accept them is to give them a warm and heartfelt smile. This applies to total strangers, even someone very unlike you in dress or accomplishments or appearance. If I smile and nod my head at a stranger I pass on the street, I've recognized and accepted him in just that moment.

Acceptance is more than tolerance. Tolerance is just putting up with someone. Acceptance implies respect. You are telling that person "you have the right to be just who you are."

If you don't feel like smiling, it will require practice and sincerity of purpose towards other people. There are times when other people are not very likable and that's when they need a smile the most. A smile is powerful enough to change another person's attitude in an instant.

Approval

Beyond acceptance, we crave approval. Relationships, personalities and work environments are damaged and destroyed by the disapproval of destructive negative criticism. Destructive criticism eats at the very core of personality. It stimulates feeling of guilt, inferiority, unworthiness.

So-called constructive criticism—I think it's rather rare in actual practice—is the act of correcting somebody's behavior by giving them instructions on how to change it. Constructive criticism is sometimes necessary with children, employees, or students.

Destructive criticism tears down the other person's self-esteem with statements like *You never clean up your room...you never finish what you start... you're always late.* Occasionally the critic will try to disguise the negative energy with "constructive" statements such as *You didn't finish the job again. You've got to stick with it.*

Rarely does anyone change as the result of destructive criticism. You just lower their self-esteem and make them hostile to you. You might as well shoot yourself in the foot, particularly if you're criticizing a family member or employee.

Here's a process that I've discovered to criticize constructively and express approval of the other person at the same time.

In my classes we have a strenuous exercise known as mountain climbers. Often when a student is struggling or doing them improperly, I will walk over and say "Your mountain climbers are perfect. I just want you to change one thing. Bring your knees up a little higher." The student feels that they have been stroked or complimented instead of criticized.

They remember the change because they've experienced approval. "I'm doing great but now I can do even better if I make that one little change."

I can live for two months on a good compliment.

—Mark Twain

Often if you compliment others on all the things they do well, while not mentioning what they do poorly, the positively reinforced behavior will get stronger and more frequent, while the ignored behavior will decrease. This process works especially well with children.

Approval of others means you build them up rather than tear them down. If you must criticize, first say something positive, then make your criticism short and to the point. Keep it in the present tense, because people can't change the past and there's no point in making them feel guilty.

Finish up your critique with another statement of approval: "Those mountain climbers look great! Keep up the good work."

Admiration

The founder of Mary Kay Cosmetics said that one of the reasons for her tremendous success was that "I pretend that everyone I meet has a sign hanging around their neck that says *make me feel important.*" It wasn't that she had a better product or more business knowledge, it was that people were more willing to help her because she made them feel important.

People sometimes mistakenly believe that there's not enough power to go around. "If I shrink someone's else's importance," they reason, "it will make me look more important, more esteemed." That attitude is exactly the opposite of how the world works.

The law of reciprocation states that it is impossible to make someone else feel important without also making yourself feel important to the same degree. Raising someone else's self-esteem raises your own in exactly the same proportion.

Praise is one of the most effective ways of making others feel important. Not the insincere flattery that is meant to manipulate, but genuine expressions of admiration for what others have accomplished in their lives.

Giving praise is an art form in itself. It will reinforce positive behavior in children, particularly. Ken Blanchard, author of "The One Minute Manager," recommends the use of one-minute praising throughout the day. Catch people doing something right and comment on it. The more that you praise, the more effective and competent they feel and the more likely they are to repeat the behavior that has won the praise. Nothing has greater power to raise someone's self-esteem than a sincere expression of approval.

> *The deepest principle in human nature is the craving to be appreciated.*
> —William James

All great leaders, all great managers understand the art of praising. True leaders are masters at getting people to cooperate with them because those people feel good about themselves. Praise is a powerful motivator. Napoleon discovered that men won't go to battle for money, but will die for ribbons and praise.

Some tips for effective praise:

- Be immediate. Praise loses its impact the longer you wait.

- Be specific with your praise. Saying *you're a great kid,* or *you're doing a great job* will have a moderate impact, but doesn't mention the specific action that you want repeated. Specific praise is: *I loved the way you closed that sale.*

- Praise in public. Criticize in private.

Don't forget to also give yourself a pat on the back and express approval for what you do. I often reward myself for something praiseworthy with a wonderful meal at my favorite Chinese restaurant or by buying myself a present.

Attitude of Gratitude

The happiest people are those who go through their lives being genuinely grateful for the things that happen to them. I am eternally grateful to the man who saved my life in Vietnam. I am very grateful to the people who have helped me grow and achieve my goals throughout my life, with nothing to gain for themselves. I still express appreciation to them in my speeches. As insignificant as what they did at the time may have seemed to them, they have been instrumental in helping me overcome tremendous hurdles, especially hurdles in self-image and overcoming doubts, so I thank them continually.

Don't wait till Thanksgiving to be thankful. Be thankful everyday. One religious writer stated that, if you only say one prayer during your entire life, it should be *Thank you.*

What Brian Tracy calls an attitude of gratitude also guarantees a healthy personality. Numerous studies have shown that people with negative attitudes have weaker immune systems and get sick more often.

Take a look around you. Negative people are always complaining and never look healthy. I am always being told I have boundless energy. It comes from having an attitude of gratitude, from being positive.

The more thankful you are for what you have, the more you will receive to be thankful for. Expressing appreciation for something someone has done or said requires two simple words "Thank you." They are two of the most powerful words in any language.

Thank people for their generosity, their help, their time. Say thank you to your spouse. People that look up to you, such as your children, are especially reactive to your gratitude.

Even when children have assigned chores around the house, it does not relieve parents from saying "thank you." Appreciate the thoroughness, appreciate the promptness, appreciate the attention to detail.

I say thank you for business appointments. I thank them for their time even before I've used it, then I thank them again afterwards. They always respond with "any time you need me, just call."

For those of you in sales, the first thing you should do is thank the person for giving you their time.

A thank you note, often forgotten in an era of e-mail, will set you apart from the crowd. A simple written expression of thanks can be treasured for a month or for years.

171

These are not "pie-in-the-sky" ways to get along with others. Human potential has been studied and researched exhaustively from virtually every direction.

Whether you read Thomas Moore's "Care of the Soul," or Brian Tracy's "Maximum Achievement," you are studying ways to grow into your own inner power. Everything we become in life is expressed from the inner self. Your progress affects the rest of the world. The development of the human soul is at the leading edge of 21st century technology.

I don't know about you, but I don't want to spend the rest of my life exactly as I am today. I want to grow, discover my inner possibilities and challenge my abilities to make them real. This means I must change. I must face that inevitable, scary world of change. I must control the direction of change by setting goals, then manage change's impact on my life. Ultimately I must embrace change as the great truth...the true path to power.

Life is dancing before you. Don't wait any longer.

Pil Sung!

Your Path to Power:
A Workbook

It matters not how strait the gate,
How charged with punishments the scroll,
I am the master of my fate:
I am the captain of my soul.
—William Henley

It's time now for you to get very specific about your own life. Think about the crises and challenges that confront you. What are you going to do about them?

Reading this book may motivate or inspire you, but it's no substitute for action. The solution to all the problems and crises that you encounter in life is inside you. You may discover how to achieve your dreams and your desires by writing answers to the questions that follow.

Writing answers rather than thinking them is essential to the process. When you write, a more natural flow occurs from the unconscious mind. You're more likely to stay on subject, and to express hidden thoughts and memories that suddenly spring to mind.

One writer referred to it as an underground stream of images and reflections. Ideas and goals need to be committed to paper as evidence to our mind that they are "real." A fleeting inspiration that is not written down will probably be lost tomorrow.

One important warning: Do not use these writing exercises as a delaying tactic for the real work that lies ahead of you. As soon as you have clearly formulated your goals and know what you want, *BEGIN*. Continue the writing process to fine-tune your plans and attitudes and ideas as you move along. Later, you can even rewrite some of your plans. Note how many of your goals you have already accomplished as you continue to rewrite and refine your plans.

If you commit yourself to these goals and set yourself in motion, Providence will move right along with you. Unseen forces will come to your aid. Unforeseen circumstances, meetings, and assistance will present themselves to you. Remember the words of Goethe. Paste these words to your mirror and read them every morning:

Whatever you can do,
or dream you can,
begin it.
Boldness
has genius, power
and magic in it.

For your writing practice, use three separate notebooks.

Label the first notebook: **Family and Personal Relationships**. This is the most essential part of your life. This is *why* you reach for your goals. Eighty-five percent of your happiness in life will come from these relationships.

Label the second notebook: **Career and Professional Life**. This is *how* you achieve your goals, both the financial security that brings peace of mind as well as the self-esteem that results naturally from knowing you're good at what you do.

Label the third notebook: **Self-Improvement**. This is *what* you do to reach your goals. This is the area of spiritual growth and mental attitude that makes a successful and happy life possible.

Answer the following questions in each one of those notebooks. Leave room after each of the following sections for later additions. This will become a journal of your progress and you may want to review it or add to it as you go along.

Setbacks

1. What challenges are facing me in this area of my life?
2. What setbacks or crises have affected me in the last year?
3. What circumstances do I wish to change?
4. What have I done so far to surmount these difficulties? Has it worked?

Taking on life

1. Write down three to five goals you want to achieve in this area of your life. Think of something you haven't done yet. Something that will change your life. Begin today.
2. What knowledge do I need to acquire to reach these goals?
3. What actions are necessary to achieve these goals?
4. Am I committed? Am I willing to do whatever it takes?

Preparing for a quantum leap

1. Are there any old rules or mottoes that I live by, even though they are no longer working?
2. What will I risk if I go for my goals?
3. What will I risk if I don't try to achieve my goals?
4. What assumptions have I made about my own limitations?
5. In what areas of my life have I "failed" in the past? Was this failure permanent?
6. In which goal area would a quantum leap now be possible? Am I willing to embrace immediate change?

The power of attitude

1. What are my own spiritual beliefs and values? How are these reflected in my attitude?
2. What are my expectations for myself? Do I expect that I will eventually fail or succeed at my goals?
3. Am I following my dreams or am I now doing something that I really don't want to do?
4. Are my closest associates positive or negative in their attitudes? How do their attitudes affect me?
5. How determined am I to reach these goals? Am I willing to do more than try? Am I willing to do whatever it takes?
6. What more can I do that I haven't already done?
7. A specific circumstance in which I can "act as if" I have a positive attitude (whether I do or not) would be:

Peace of mind by eliminating fear and anger.

1. What fear is holding me back from going after my goals?
2. What action can I take to face this fear?
3. In what way can I actually move towards my fear?
4. Am I often angry? Do I usually blame some other person or event for my temper outbursts?
5. The next time I feel myself becoming angry, what method will I use to slow myself down and acquire patience? (Consult chapter 5 for ideas)
6. How can I let go of my anger? What grudges am I carrying against other people? What action would demonstrate my forgiveness?

Staying hungry

1. What do I love to do with all my heart and soul? What would I be willing to do even if I were never paid?
2. What do I find easy that others find hard? What have others told me I'm good at?
3. How badly do I want to achieve my goals? Do I wish I could do it, or am I willing to do whatever it takes? What is the most this goal could require of me?
4. What excuses have I given myself or others for not already accomplishing my goal? Are these valid reasons or simply excuses?
5. What will it feel like to accomplish my goal? What will I feel like when I am already in that situation?
6. How often do I think about my goals and ideals? Are they an occasional wishful thought or do they fill every spare moment?
7. Am I willing to trust in the unseen forces that will come to my assistance? Have I seen any evidence of Providence working in my favor already?

Quantum learning

1. In what ways do I keep a full cup by assuming I already know all I need to know about a subject or person?
2. Three ways in which I can gain new knowledge about how to achieve my goal by approaching with an empty cup are.........
3. Three ways I can improve my listening skills are...........

What's important now?

1. What steps will take me closer to my goals?
2. What needs to be done right now?
3. Three ways that I can keep myself in the present today are............

Cooperating with life

1. Am I frequently hard on myself? Do I punish myself with guilt when I don't live up to my own expectations?
2. Do I often catch myself complaining or agreeing with other complainers?
3. Three particular instances in which I was disappointed with my behavior recently were......
4. Here is how I will behave or respond differently next time these situations occur.....

Dealing with doctors and other experts

1. What do I need to discuss with a doctor or other expert in order to achieve my goal?
2. Do I need more than one opinion?
3. Have I educated myself?
4. Do I know my own mind and body or am I merely believing what I want to believe?
5. How can I find someone else who may have already accomplished my goal who may be willing to give me advice?

Women

1. What is my ideal self like?
2. What is my self-image?
3. Do I believe I am worth fighting for?
4. Affirmations I will use daily to pledge my willingness to fight for myself are........
5. Ways in which I can learn self-defense techniques or other ways of fighting for myself are.......

Men

1. How do I express my personal power and aggression in relationship to my goals? Is this expression positive or negative?
2. If I need someone else's help in achieving my goals and desires, how can I ask them or compensate them in such a way that it respects their self-interest?
3. Ways in which I can bring a better attitude to this goal area are........
4. Ways in which I can exercise more responsibility in my life are......
5. If it's to be, it's up to me. How can I achieve my own happiness?

Loving myself

1. Do I accept myself the way I am? Do I try to deny aspects of my character or personality that I know aren't too likable?
2. Today I will listen for any negative self-talk and use affirmations to reprogram my subconscious. These affirmations are........
3. I resolve not to be sorry, but to be better. Ways in which I can forgive myself for past behavior are......
4. Ways in which I can "act as if" I am a confident, self-accepting person are.....
5. Are my daily actions and thoughts congruent with my spiritual values? In what areas can I demonstrate more integrity in my behavior?

6. Is there anything in my life now that I need to take a stand on? What values will I use in taking that stand?

Loving others

1. How committed am I to my relationships? Is there a way I can increase my commitment level to 100%?
2. Am I afraid for any reason? Does this fear cause me to behave in a jealous, possessive or controlling manner?
3. In what ways can I improve my own behavior within the context of this relationship?
4. What are my partners good qualities? How can I express these to him or her?
5. Are the lines of communication open? Do I listen sincerely? Do I make my own thoughts and needs known?
6. Three loving acts of kindness that I can do today to rekindle this relationship are........

Loving the world

1. Ways in which I can be more agreeable in my interactions with other people are.....
2. Ways in which I can practice acceptance of others are......
3. Ways in which I can express more approval are.....
4. Ways in which I can express more admiration for those around me are.......
5. People, circumstances, talents and gifts in my life for which I am thankful are.......
6. Ways in which I can give something back are.........

About the Authors

Mack Newton is a sought-after motivational speaker who appears regularly on television and radio, as well as being the subject of numerous newspaper and magazine articles. Mack is a health and fitness consultant, rehabilitative specialist, body conditioning expert, a seventh degree black belt and a two-time World Champion in Taekwon-Do. He is ranked as a master Taekwon-Do instructor, one of only a handful in the United States. In 1995, he was inducted into the World Martial Arts Hall of Fame.

Mack Newton has become known as "The Champion's Champion" for his work with athletes such as Bo Jackson, Neil Lomax, Jay Novacek, Seth Joyner, Anaeas Williams and Roy Green. He was conditioning coach for the Oakland A's for nine years and the Dallas Cowboys for three years, and continues to serve as consultant for top athletic teams across the nation.

As President and CEO of NTKD Rehabilitative Services, Inc. in Phoenix, Arizona, he continues to motivate peak performance in clients from four years of age to eighty. In addition to athletes, Mack coaches people with debilitating arthritis, hip replacement or other joint trauma, and injuries due to surgery or auto accidents. He inspires those who have endured crisis and defeat to empower themselves, to relish life, and realize their dreams.

Michele St. George is an award-winning freelance writer who has published over 150 articles in such magazines as *Woman's Day, Mature Outlook, American Health* and *Entrepreneur.* She is also co-author of the book *The Shaman Bulldog,* released by Warner Books in 1996.

181

Order Form

	Qty	Cost Each	Total
A Path to Power $14.95			
Accent on Excellence Four audio cassettes on Self-Acceptance, Self-Esteem, Quantum Thinking, Integrity, Goal Setting, and Becoming a Winner. $49.95			
I Will Fight Back: Self-Defense for Women Four videotapes of Mack Newton's workshop. Includes techniques and variations of physical and psychological responses to an attack. The course stresses total awareness of surroundings, prevention of attacks, and the many tools available to control a situation. This program is appropriate for everyone, regardless of age, size, or level of physical fitness. $59.95			
Total Order:			
Sales Tax (AZ only)			
Shipping: $3 for 1 item; $5 for 2 items; $7 for 3-5 items; $10 for 6-10 items			

☐ Check here to have your copy autographed by Mack Newton

SHIP TO:

Name _____

Address _____

City_____ State_____ Zip_____

Quantity discounts are available to groups and organizations. Write or call NTKD Publishing for details

METHOD OF PAYMENT:

___Check ___MO/Cash ___Visa ___Mastercard

Credit Card Number_____

Expiration Date ____Month _____Year

Signature_____

Mail your order
(or fax with credit
card information) to:
**NTKD Publishing,
3243-A E. Indian School Rd.
Phoenix AZ 85018**
(602) 957-6492
Fax: (602) 957-4424